SHORT CIR(

IN AND AROUNI

CW00705024

PAT T.

28 WALKS OF 3 TO 6 MILES

Follow the Countryside code

1) Be safe and plan ahead and follow any signs
2) Keep dogs under control
3) Prevent uncontrolled moorland fires
4) Protect plants and animals, take your litter home
5) Leave gates and property as you find them
6) Consider other people
7) Beware mineshafts! Derbyshire alone has over 100,000 mine shafts. Keep away from depressions in the ground in the mining areas of the Peak District. Several of the walks in this book pass through mining areas, so stay on rights of way at all times.

Published by **Ashbourne Editions**
The Oaks, Moor Farm Road West, Ashbourne, Derbyshire, DE6 1HD
Tel: (01335) 347349
Fax: (01335) 347303

ISBN: 978-1-873775-35-6

Printed by: Gomer Press, Llandysul, Ceredigion, Wales

Design & reproduction by: Mark Titterton (Ceiba Graphics)

Acknowledgements: The author wishes to thank her husband, Peter, for
all his assistance and encouragement in compiling this book, and to Roma
Wilcock for her companionship on many of the walks.

Front cover: Tissington (© Mark Titterton / ceibagraphics.co.uk)
Back cover: View of Parkhouse Hill
Opposite page: The Roaches

SHORT CIRCULAR WALKS

IN AND AROUND THE WHITE PEAK

PAT TIDSALL

28 WALKS OF 3 TO 6 MILES

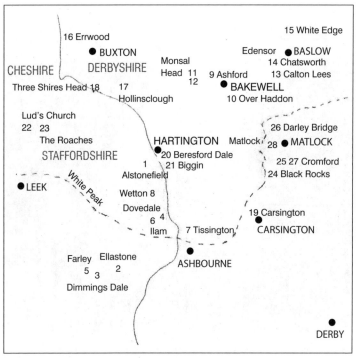

LOCATION MAP & KEY (OPPOSITE)

All the walks start at recognised car parks unless stated otherwise in the detailed walk descriptions.

Sheepwash Bridge, Ashford-in-the-Water

	Roads		Woods
	Tracks: Drives		Rock Outcrops
	Railways	✝	Church
	Trails	▲	Youth Hostel
	The Route	F B	Footbridge
	Rivers	C. P.	Car Park
	Lakes	P. H.	Public House: Inns

WALK INDEX

WALK	AREA	DISTANCE	GRADE	PAGE
ASHBOURNE				
Walk 1	Alstonefield, Dovedale and Milldale	3 ½ miles	2★	10
Walk 2	Calwich Park and Ellastone	6 miles	2	12
Walk 3	Dimmings Dale and The Staffordshire Moorlands Walks	3 miles	1	16
Walk 4	Dovedale and Bunster Hill	5 miles	2★	17
Walk 5	Farley and The Churnet Valley	6 miles	2	20
Walk 6	Ilam and Thorpe	4 miles	2	23
Walk 7	Tissington	3 miles	1	26
Walk 8	Wetton and The Manifold Way	5 miles	3★	27
BAKEWELL				
Walk 9	Ashford-in-the-Water and Monsal Head	4 miles	2	30
Walk 10	Bakewell and Over Haddon	6 miles	2	33
Walk 11	Monsal Head and Monsal Dale	3 ½ miles	3	36
Walk 12	Monsal Head and Rowland	5 miles	1	38
BASLOW				
Walk 13	Calton Lees and Rowsley	5 miles	2	40
Walk 14	Chatsworth and Edensor	5 miles	2	42
Walk 15	White Edge and Froggatt Edge	6 miles	2	44

WALK	AREA	DISTANCE	GRADE	PAGE
BUXTON				
Walk 16	Errwood Reservoir	4 ½ miles	2	46
Walk 17	Hollinsclough and Chrome Hill	4 ½ miles	3★	49
Walk 18	Three Shire Heads and The Dane Valley	6 miles	3	52
CARSINGTON				
Walk 19	Carsington and Hopton	5 ½ miles	2	55
HARTINGTON				
Walk 20	Hartington and Beresford Dale	3 ½ miles	1	58
Walk 21	Hartington and Biggin Dale	3 miles	1	60
LEEK				
Walk 22	Lud's Church (to the North West of The Roaches)	3 miles	1★	62
Walk 23	The Roaches	4 miles	2★	64
MATLOCK				
Walk 24	Black Rocks and Wirksworth	4 ½ miles	3★	66
Walk 25	Cromford and High Peak Trail	5 ½ miles	2	69
Walk 26	Darley Bridge and Wensley Dale	4 miles	1	72
Walk 27	High Peak Junction and Cromford Canal	5 miles	2	74
Walk 28	Matlock and Bonsall	5 miles	3★	77

INTRODUCTION

Derbyshire is not only the Peak District. The scenery outside the Peak National Park is equally impressive. The dramatic landscape around the Matlock area and the rolling hills and valleys south of Chesterfield are all delightful walking areas and are less crowded than the Peak Park.

The 22 circular walks in this book cover an area from Castleton in the north to Tissington in the southwest and Ambergate in the southeast. Five of the walks are outside the Peak District. Within the Peak National Park I have included Edge, Dale and moorland walks.

By the very nature of the county all walks will have hills of varying length and steepness. All the walks are suitable for the reasonably fit walker. To help evaluate the walks they are graded according to the total height climbed.

1. Grade 1: less than 300ft; with some flat sections for the less able walker and wheelchairs.

2. Grade 2: 300ft to 600ft.

3. Grade 3: 600ft to 1000ft.

Other information provided:-

1. ★ These stars indicate difficult sections of the route, such as ascents, descents or terrain.
2. Stiles:- **S** - 1 to 10, **SS** - 10 to 20, **SSS** - over 20.
3. The distance is given to the nearest half mile.
4. The approximate time is for reasonably fit walkers and does not allow for stops. It is estimated that the average continuous walking time is 2 miles per hour.
5. The two maps recommended for these walks are: Explorer OL24, and Explorer OL259.
6. Parking is given with the Grid Ref. and in most cases is at a public car park. This is the start of the walk. On a few walks you may have to park on the roadside or in a layby. Please ensure that gates and roads are not blocked and that other vehicles can pass safely.

7. Refreshment and picnic areas are suggested but please bear in mind that they are not recommendations as the former can change hands and picnic areas may change.

8. An indication is given for each walk if there are suitable stretches for the less able walker.

The countryside is not static and changes may have taken place between the research for these walks and their publication. Please note that the directions given in the route instructions are as you stand with your back to the stile or gate.

There can be swiftly changing weather conditions in this whole area. It can be different up on the moorlands and hillsides as against the valleys. Please always be aware of the latest weather forecast and have suitable clothing and footwear. You will notice that the maps in the book are only intended as a guide to the route. We consider it advisable always to carry the relevant O.S. map.

WALK 1

Alstonefield, Dovedale and Milldale

Alstonefield, Gipsy Bank, Dovedale, Lode Mill, Pinch Beck, Milldale, Alstonefield

Map: Explorer OL 24 White Peak

Parking: Grid Ref SK 131556

Distance: 3 ½ miles

Approx. Time: 2 ½ hours

Grade: 2*

Paths: Tracks, dale and field paths

Stiles: SS

Refreshments: Alstonefield and Milldale snack bar

Picnic: Milldale by the river with the ducks!

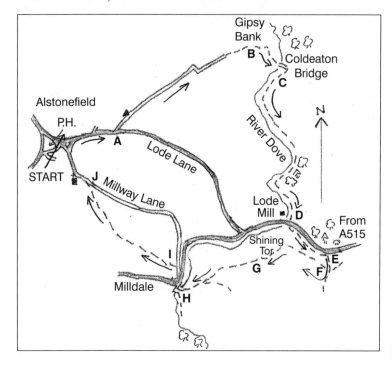

Directions

From Ashbourne take the A515 Buxton Road. In 5 ½ miles turn left to Alstonefield. Follow the minor road for nearly 3 miles crossing the River Dove. There are two car parks in the village, both clearly marked. The walk starts at The George Inn car park entrance.

Description

A walk of great contrasts where you follow upland field paths and tracks with wide open views and deep valley paths along the beautiful River Dove with steep limestone cliffs. There are two very steep climbs each of which will take about 5 minutes.

Route Instructions

1. From wherever you park, walk back to the entrance of The George Inn car park. Continue ahead to follow the Lode Mill and Ashbourne routes.

2. In about 400 metres turn left at the second track signed Youth Hostel. {A}

3. Follow the well-used track then path to the head of Gipsy Bank.

4. Cross the stile and bearing slightly right, walk down the very steep bank {B} to cross Coldeaton Bridge.

5. Turn right along the path with the River Dove on the right. Go through a squeeze stile by an old gate.

6. {C} Follow the riverside path for 15 to 20 minutes crossing four squeeze stiles. Pass the cottages on the left and Lode Mill on the right to climb steps to the bridge. {D}

7. (If you want an easy ½ mile route to Milldale turn right across the bridge then immediately left along a minor road by the river. For the more strenuous rewarding route turn left.)

8. Cross the road diagonally left to go through a small gate into the National Trust area of Shining Tor. Follow the alternative route avoiding the road. Cross two stiles round a rock outcrop. At the signpost turn right signed "Tissington 2 ½ m". {E}

9. Climb up the steep Pinch Bank (about 5 minutes). At the top turn right by the footpath post to follow the "Milldale ¾ m" route. {F}

10. Keep a wall over on the left as you admire the wonderful views. In ½ mile cross a wall stile ahead. {G} You now have the wall on the right as you descend the hillside. Shortly you will see a wall and a gateway on the left. Follow this wall as you bear round to the right where you will see the start of a narrow path winding downhill quite steeply to Milldale.

11. Cross the footbridge to the road in Milldale and turn left then immediately right.

12. Pass Polly's Cottage where you can obtain a snack. Walk up the lane for just over 50 metres. At Valley View turn left by the footpath post to go through a small metal gate. (If you do not wish to climb the next steep slope continue up the longer and less steep route to the church in Alstonefield).

13. Walk up the grass by the drive and hedge to go through a small gate in the conifer hedge.

14. Keep straight on with the field boundary over on the left. Go through a gated stile ahead. Climb the hill following the power lines and after the last power line pole in the field bear right to the top right-hand corner of the field.

15. Go through the squeeze stile and walk diagonally across the next field and through another squeeze stile. Bear round to the right up the middle of the field keeping the church over to the left.

16. Go through a stile by a farmgate and turn left. Walk along the lane passing the church and going round a right-hand bend. Walk back into the village of Alstonefield.

WALK 2
Calwich Park and Ellastone

Ellastone Car Park, B5032, Limestone Way, Middle Mayfield, River Dove, Ellastone

Map: Explorer 259 Derby and Ashbourne
Parking: Grid Ref SK 116434
Distance: 6 miles
Approx. Time: 3 ½ hours
Grade: 2
Paths: Mainly field paths and tracks
Stiles: SSS
Refreshments: Middle Mayfield "Rose and Crown" (Open 12-2pm, closed on Mondays except Bank Holidays after which no meals are served on the Tuesday)

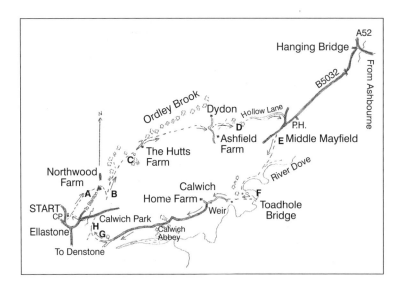

Directions

From Ashbourne take the A52 Leek road as far as the bridge over the River Dove at Hanging Bridge. Turn left here to follow the B5032 Uttoxeter road. Drive through Mayfield and Middle Mayfield to Ellastone (just over 3 miles). In Ellastone turn right where the B5032 bends round to the left, signed Wootton. In a few metres turn right at the car park sign and left into the car park opposite the church.

Description

This area of Staffordshire outside the White Peak is very peaceful and would make a good Bank Holiday walk away from some of the more popular areas of the White Peak. The walk is relatively easy across undulating farmland with far reaching views to the Weaver Hills. The return route follows paths and tracks in the River Dove valley. Most of the way is well marked with "Countryside Care" signs.

The dogs at Hutts Farm were friendly when we stopped and "spoke" to them!

Route Instructions

1. From the car park leave via the main entrance and turn right. In a few metres turn left through a gate to walk round the churchyard. Go through another small gate signed "Weaver Walk".

2. Bear left across the field corner to cross a stile then keep straight on following a hedge on the right and passing a house. Cross a stile in the field corner.

3. Bear right down the field to cross two drainage ditches then a stile. {A} Continue up the field aiming to the right of the farm. Cross the stile in the field corner.

4. Walk down to the minor road and turn left. Follow the road and just after passing Northwood Farm cross a wall stile by the footpath post to walk down steps.

5. Cross the farm drive diagonally left to cross another stile and down steps. Turn right downhill first with a fence on the right and at the end of it bear right again to cross a fence stile. Walk diagonally down the paddock to cross a footbridge. {B}

6. Walk up to a narrow path just ahead and turn left to aim first for a fence corner then for a farm gate ahead. Cross the stile by this gate.

7. Aim up the field for a mound and four single trees. {C} Cross the mound between the two right-hand trees and then aim for a house in the trees ahead.

8. Cross a stile by a farm gate to walk past The Hutts Farm on the right. Follow the track downhill and at the left bend leave the track to cross a stile by two farm gates.

9. Follow a fence close on the left uphill crossing a stile then keeping a fence, an old wall and a wood down on the left to cross another stile in the field corner.

10. Bear right up the field to the corner of a holly hedge then keep straight on, away from the hedge, following a grass track which you leave after a few metres to walk to a fence corner. Follow the fence then a hedge on the right.

11. Cross a stile in the field corner. (At this stile it is worth a look back at the far reaching views across to the Weaver Hills and Wootton Park where the route takes you in Walk 5)

12. You now have a conifer plantation on the left and a wall on the right.

13. Cross a squeeze stile and keep straight on then cross another squeeze stile hidden by a holly bush in the field corner.

14. Bear right across the field to and through a farm gate/gap. Turn left to have a hedge on the left. Cross the farm track ahead between Dydon and Ashfield Farm to follow the hedge close on the left. Cross the stile in the field corner (not the stile on the left). Please note, there may be an electric fence by the track. If this is the case cross the cattle grid to follow the hedge on the right then cross a stile on the right just before a farm gate. Turn left to cross the stile ahead.

15. Bear slightly right up the field and soon you will be aiming for a fence and a squeeze stile ahead. Cross the stile and turn left to cross another stile by a gate. (At this point you leave the Limestone Way)

16. Bear off right across the field aiming for the buildings in Middle Mayfield. Cross

a stile just to the left of the field corner.

17. {D} Make your way down to a rutted track and hedge on the right. Soon the track becomes more obvious as you walk through the trees. Cross a stile to continue down the track. Part of Hollow Lane could be very muddy especially after rain. Eventually you go through a gate and turn right to follow a fence on the left and pass a house. Continue down the track to the minor road in Middle Mayfield. Turn right.

18. Walk down to the B5032 and turn right again. In about 200 metres cross the stile on the left. {E}

19. Follow the hawthorn trees on the left for a few metres before bearing off right aiming for a hedge gap in the bottom corner of the field. Cross an old stile (or go through the gap!)

20. Keep straight on crossing four fields, stiles and hedge gaps.

21. At last you come to the River Dove on the left. Cross two more fields and stiles. In the third field aim for Toadhole Foot Bridge over the river.

22. {F} Do not cross the bridge but turn right back on yourself to walk at about a 45° angle away from the bridge and the path you have just walked. Aim for the tree scattered hillside between two houses. Soon you will see a single tree by a ditch in the field. Cross the right-hand end of this ditch then aim for the waymarked fence in the field corner.

23. Cross a footbridge via two stiles. Walk up to a farm track and turn right.

24. Follow this track up round the hill. As you near Calwich Home Farm ignore a track off left then at a crossing of tracks below the farm turn left.

25. Follow a track for about a mile (it is surfaced as far as the hamlet of Calwich Abbey).

26. {G} At a fork of tracks cross a stile by a farm gate to take the right-hand fork. Cross a stile then go across and round a field aiming for Ellastone church and passing an old quarry. (The large stones on top of the mound could make quite a pleasant picnic stop) {H}

27. Continue across the field to the road passing through two gates and by a cottage close on the left.

28. Turn left across the bridge and walk to the junction with the minor road to Stanton, cross this junction to cross a stile by the sheep enclosure. Walk up the field to the gate in the church wall. Retrace the path through the churchyard back to the car park.

WALK 3

Dimmings Dale and The Staffordshire Moorlands Walks

The Ramblers Retreat, Staffordshire Moorlands Walks, Oldfurnace, Stoney Dale, Ousal Dale, (Staffordshire Way) Ramblers Retreat

Map: Explorer 259 Derby, Ashbourne
Parking: SK 063431
Distance: 3 miles
Approx. Time: 1 ½ hours
Grade: 1
Paths: Lakeside and woodland paths, minor road and tracks
Stiles: None
Refreshments: Ramblers Retreat open all year

Directions

From Ashbourne take the A52 Leek road. In 4 ½ miles turn left, still on the A52 leaving the A523 Leek road. In just over 2 ½ miles turn left onto the B5417 Oakamoor road. Follow this road for 2 ¾ miles keeping straight on at a cross roads to follow the Cheadle road, still on the B5417. In Oakamoor cross the river bridge over the Churnet and almost immediately turn left along a minor road signed Ramblers Retreat. In just over ¼ mile, having ignored the "station" car park sign, turn left along Red Road signed Ramblers Retreat. In about one mile turn right into the large car park by the Ramblers Retreat.

Description

This is a lovely walk through the ever changing woodlands of Dimmings Dale. For most of the way you are on good, wide woodland tracks. The Ramblers Retreat offers snacks, teas and full meals. For parties you would need to book. 01538 702730

Route Instructions

1. From the car park walk in front of the Ramblers Retreat and take the left-hand route passing close to the fence round the garden and outdoor eating area. Follow the wide track passing by the Forestry Commission Boom.
2. Keep the lake and stream on the right. In about ¾ mile, when you reach the second lake, turn right along a path which separates the two parts of the lake.{A}
3. Turn left, the upper lake is now on the left. Follow the Staffordshire Moorlands

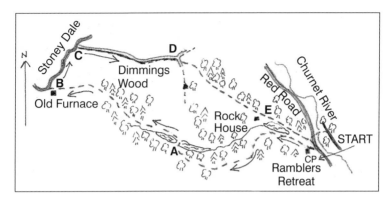

Walk for just over ¾ mile. You will pass a boom, cross a stream, pass a lake on the right, then Old Furnace Cottage on the left and lastly the stream before you reach the road at Old furnace. {B}

4. Turn right to walk up the rather steep minor twisting road (Stoney Dale). In about ¼ mile turn right to walk up a tarmac drive. {C} Follow the drive, which is still part of the Staffordshire Way, for ½ mile. At a fork in the road walk to the main Y.H.A. sign.

5. {D} Cross the cattle grid and turn left down the narrow path through open woodland of Ousal Dale. At a crossing of paths bear right to continue down the dale to Earl's Rock House. {E}

6. Continue ahead with the lake on your right.

7. After another ¼ mile you will arrive back at the car park ready for a welcome cup of tea at The Ramblers Retreat.

WALK 4

Dovedale and Bunster Hill

Dovedale Car Park, Ilam Rock, Dovedale Wood, Air Cottage, Ilamtops Farm, Ilam, Izaak Walton Hotel

Map: Explorer OL 24 White Peak
Parking: Grid Ref SK 147509
Distance: 5 miles

Approx. Time: 3 hours

Grade: 2★

Paths: Riverside, wooded hillside and field paths

Stiles: S

Refreshments: Izaak Walton Hotel and refreshment van at the car park

Picnic: Instruction 6 below Air Cottage

Directions

From Ashbourne take the A515 Buxton road turning left in about a mile. Follow the road to and through Thorpe village. Soon you will have a magnificent view over Dovedale and the Izaak Walton to Ilam. At the bottom of the hill having crossed the bridge turn right up the narrow road to the car park. SK147509.

Description

Although this walk is very challenging the views are spectacular. A clear path up from the dale is very steep as it winds up through the woods. From Air Cottage the route follows a track to just before the road. If you have the OS map OL24, and are experienced walkers, you will see that there are alternate routes to Ilam but all of them are very steep downhill paths. The climb up to Bunster Hill is steep but the views are wonderful. This would become a grade 3★ if you did the Bunster Hill route.

Route Instructions

1. Leave the car park at the northern end to follow the river on the right. Turn right to cross the footbridge. (At certain times of the year the stepping stones may well be flooded). Turn left to follow the river.

2. {A} At the stepping stones keep straight on, going through a stile, to follow the well used path up the dale. In just over a mile having climbed up over Lover's Leap, turn left at the footpath sign to cross the bridge over the river. {B}

3. Turn right by Ilam Rock to walk along the path to the footpath sign. Turn left to follow the Ilam route.

4. Walk up the very steep, partly stepped, winding path through Dovedale Wood. In about 20 minutes, near the top, ignore a stile on the right to continue ahead on an undulating path, walking parallel to the dale below.

5. Leave the wood via a small gate to keep straight on across the hillside walking below the farm buildings. After passing a footpath post the path becomes more rocky and undulating.

6. At the next footpath post turn right. Walk up the hill passing the waymarked post

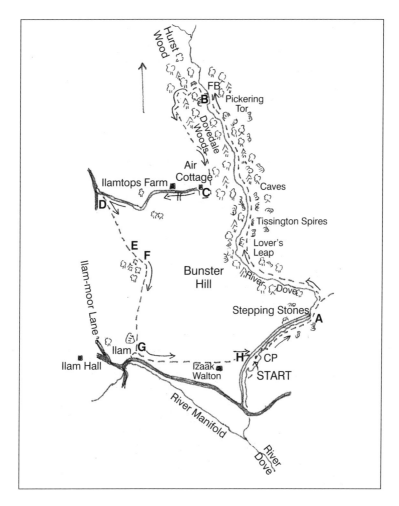

to go through two small gates by Air Cottage. {C}.

7. Turn left along a track for about ½ mile, cross a cattle grid then through a gateway to pass Ilamtops Farm.

8. At the end of the track and just before the gateway onto the road turn left to cross a wall stile to the right of a gate/gateway. {D}

9. Keep straight on aiming for the left-hand end of open woodland. Cross the stile onto Access land. {E} Keep the wall and wood over to your right as you walk quite steeply downhill. The wall soon bends away right as you aim for the western slopes of Bunster Hill. Go through a gate in the wall ahead. {F}

10. Turn right still descending steeply aiming for the lake on the right and keeping a wall over to the right. Soon you will be on a farm track with the wall close on the right. At a T-junction of tracks, turn left. {G}

11. Follow the track to go through a stile. Continue ahead crossing the fields and stiles and gate towards the woods of Dovedale and passing The Izaak Walton Hotel on your right.

12. {H} Cross a stile and down steps to walk through the overflow Dovedale car park.

WALK 5

Farley and The Churnet Valley

Dimmings Dale Car Park, Lord's Bridge, Barbary Gutter, Farley, Wootton Park, Churnet Valley

Map: Explorer 259 Derby and Ashbourne
Parking: SK Grid Ref SK 063431
Distance: 6 miles.
Approx. Time: 3 to 3 ½ hours
Grade: 2
Paths: Woodland paths and tracks, estate roads, dismantled railway (Churnet Valley)
Stiles: SS
Refreshments: Ramblers Retreat

Directions

See Walk 3 Dimmings Dale and Staffordshire Moorlands Walks

Description

This is a really lovely walk especially in the spring when the rhododendrons are in bloom. The route starts up the gentle climb through Barbary Gutter passing the Chained Oak. Field paths take you to Farley, then paths and estate roads through Wootton Park where there are far reaching views as well as deer and the wonderful

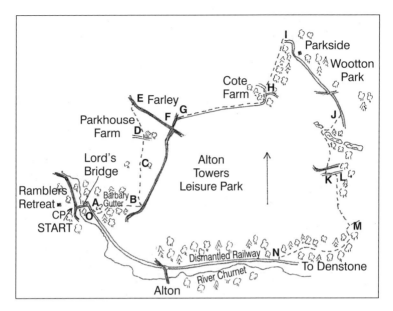

display of rhododendrons. The last mile is along the pretty trail of the old railway track in the Churnet Valley.

Route Instructions

1. From the car park entrance cross the road bearing slightly left. Turn right to go through the small gate by a farm gate. Cross Lord's Bridge over the River Churnet and the disused railway.

2. {A} Turn right along the wide woodland path ignoring all paths off. Follow this meandering track up through the woods of Barbary Gutter. (You will pass steps up to the huge Chained Oak)

3. {B} As you come out of the wood near the road turn sharp left then right by the entrance to a B&B at The Chained Oak. Go through a narrow gap and turn left to cross a stile.

4. Keep straight on to pass a large hawthorn tree on your right. Now aim for a single pine tree between two stands of pine trees on the ridge. Once on the ridge aim for the fence stile slightly down to your right. Cross the stile and bear slightly left aiming to the right of the largest oak tree. Walk down a slightly sunken path to a metal farm gate and a footpath sign. {C}

5. Go through a gate then follow the fence close on the right up the next field. Go through another farm gate ahead and across a track by Parkhouse Farm. {D} Cross a fence stile and bear left up towards a cream barn in Farley village. Cross two stiles by a barn and track to walk up a narrow fenced path to the road.

6. {E} Turn right along the road through Farley hamlet passing the hall. In just over ¼ mile and near the road junction and entrance to Alton Towers turn left along Longshaw Lane. {F}

7. In nearly 150 metres, at the start of a low wall with a waymarked sign, bear off right. {G}

8. Follow the wooded path downhill and then a track for about 5 minutes to join the estate road. Cross a cattle grid on to the estate road.

9. Continue ahead for nearly another 5 minutes to pass Cote Farm and Wootton estate office. Follow the estate drive which bends round to the left. Leave the driveway to turn left uphill by the footpath sign. Where the track bends left turn right to go through a fence gap by a farm gate. {H} Follow a steep fenced path up through the wood, then along the edge of the wood by the deer fence.

10. {I} Join the estate drive via a stile and a farm gate on the right. Keep straight on down the drive which soon bends round to the right by a fenced cattle grid. Follow the drive up and round Parkside. In just over 1/4 mile from Parkside keep straight on at a crossing of estate roads. Leave the drive by the footpath sign and a single oak tree on the right. {J}

11. Cross the stile to follow a fence and trees on the right. Cross the next stile in the field corner and keep straight on down to cross another stile on the right. Continue in the same direction down to another estate road.

12. Turn right then left to cross the bridge over the lakes. Turn left again to walk uphill. This is a beautiful area of azaleas and rhododendrons.

13. At the top of the hill bear off left crossing a stile below Lower Ground Farm. Keep straight on down the field and over a stile. Walk up through the bluebell wood to go through the metal gate. Cross a minor road, then on up to a track. {K}

14. Turn left along the track for about 200 metres. Just before a clearing on the left turn right up steps, leaving the track. {L} Follow the quite steep path up the edge of the wood. As you reach the top you will have a high fence on the right. In about 10 minutes from the track and just after the end of a high fence, you come to a crossing of paths. Turn right over a broken fence by the old squeeze stile. {M}

15. Walk along a short path to a wider track and turn right uphill. At the junction with another track turn left. (Notice the large stone gate posts on your right)

16. Walk down this wide woodland track ignoring a track off right. Notice the towering rocks of Ina's Rock in the trees on your right. In about ¾ mile (12 minutes), just before green metal gates, turn left down to the disused railway track. Turn right along this track. {N}

17. Follow the track for just over a mile (30 minutes) passing under one bridge at Alton station. (If the track is very wet you can follow a woodland path to the left of the old station wall)

18. {O} Just before the second bridge turn right off the track up a short path, then turn left to retrace your outward route via Lord's Bridge, back to the car park.

WALK 6
Ilam and Thorpe

Ilam National Trust Car Park, Manifold River, Coldwall Bridge, Thorpe, Thorpe Mill Farm, Dovedale Car Park, Izaak Walton Hotel, Ilam

Map: Explorer OL24 White Peak and 259 Derby and Ashbourne
Parking: Grid Ref. SK 131506
Distance: 4 miles
Approx. Time: 2 hours
Grade: 2
Paths: Field and river-side paths, tracks and minor roads
Stiles: SS
Refreshments: Izaak Walton Hotel and Ilam Hall National Trust Tea Rooms (Jul & Aug open all week; Sep, Oct, Mar to Jun open Mon, Tue & weekends; Nov, Dec, Jan & Feb open weekends)
Picnic: Instruction 7 on Coldwall Bridge
Toilets: Ilam Hall and Dovedale car park

Directions

Follow the directions in Walk 4 but at the bottom of the hill after crossing the bridge keep straight on along the road following Ilam signs. When you enter the village turn right at the monument and where the road bends to the right keep straight on towards the hall and car park.

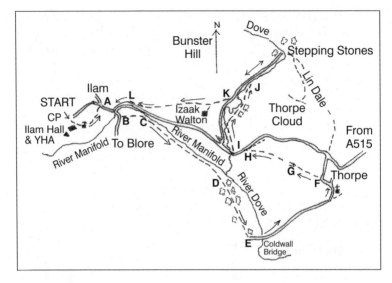

Description

The views along this walk are splendid and well worth the ascents and descents. The easy riverside paths follow first the Manifold then the Dove. A fairly steep climb brings you to the pretty village of Thorpe before you descend back to the picturesque village of Ilam where you will have time to call at the visitor centre and tea rooms.

Route Instructions

1. From the car park walk back down to the drive then continue down a path to pass the church on your right. Turn left along a drive to the road in Ilam.

2. {A} Turn right to walk along the road passing the monument on the left and crossing the bridge over the River Manifold, then immediately turn left down steps and over a stile. {B}

3. {C} Follow the riverside path crossing three stiles and two small bridges.

4. Near open woodland cross a stile by a footpath post, {D} and turn left.

5. Walk up through the open woodland following the waymarked posts (this could be quite muddy). As the wood thins out you will pass a footpath post then aim for the next footpath post.

6. Continue downhill to a farm track and then through a farm gate. Aim for the small stand of trees down to your left.

7. {E} Cross a stile by a farm gate to walk across Coldwall Bridge over the River Dove.

8. Walk up the track to Thorpe village (10 to 15 minutes) ignoring the footpath off left.

9. At the top of the track go through a farm gate/gateway. Walk through the village passing the Old Rectory and the church on the right. Keep straight on along Digmire Lane. At the Manor House and a bend in the road turn left by a footpath post. {F}

10. Go through a squeeze stile to follow the narrow walled path then through a small gate.

11. Keep straight on across the field to cross a track via two stiles and two gates. Continue ahead crossing two fields a stile and a gate.

12. Walk along a short track passing a cottage {G} to go through two farm gates.

13. Keep straight on aiming to the left of The Izaak Walton Hotel ahead. Go through a small gate between two trees in the wall ahead. Walk on down the steep field to the farm and the footpath post. {H}

14. Turn left to cross the cattle grid and on down the road passing Thorpe Mill Farm. Just before the bridge over the River Dove turn right. {I} Keeping a fence on the right, follow a grass path for a few metres to go through a gate on the right and turn left.

15. Follow the stream on the left to go through a small gate. You now have the Dove on the left. After the next gate and planked path bear right to a wood corner and fence to go through the end of the fence.

16. The wooded riverside path now follows the river again crossed by a stile and gate. At the end of the path cross a stile and turn left across the footbridge over the River Dove. {J}

(If you wish to extend your walk by a mile in all to the stepping stones turn right, then retrace your steps back to this point)

17. Turn left to walk to the car park entrance {K} opposite here you cross a stile and walk up the surfaced drive to go up steps then on up a wide track to cross the double stiles.

18. Keep straight on, passing The Izaak Walton on the left, to cross two fields and stiles, in the third field bear slightly left to go through a gate in the field corner. Continue ahead to cross a stile by a gate.

19. Walk down the farm track for about 150 metres bear off left down to and through a gate. {L}

20. Turn right to walk to the monument then turn right again to retrace your outward route.

WALK 7
Tissington

Tissington Trail Car Park and village, Field paths, Tissington Trail, Tissington Trail Car Park

Map: Explorer OL 24 White Peak

Parking: Grid Ref: SK178521

Distance: 3 miles

Approx. Time: 1 ½ hours

Grade: 1

Paths: Field paths and trail

Stiles: S

Refreshments: The Coach House in the village (Limited opening times in the winter)

Directions

From Ashbourne take the A515 Buxton road. In nearly 3 miles turn right to Tissington. Drive through the gateway over the cattle grid and down The Avenue. In the village keep straight on passing the duck pond on the right. As you leave the village turn right down to Tissington Trail Car Park.

Description

This is a short easy walk with wonderful views that will give you the time to explore Tissington village. In May {Ascension Day} the well dressings are blessed. These are well worth a visit!

Route Instructions

1. Leave the car park via the main entrance. {A} Turn left back into the village. Pass the duck pond on your left then turn right to walk up the main road through the village passing The Coach House Tea Rooms and Tissington Hall.

2. Keep straight on up and out of the village ignoring all side roads and paths. In about 150 metres, where the road bends left up Rakes Lane keep straight on. {B}

3. Follow the walled track to cross a stile by a farm gate. Keeping the wall on your left across the field and passing a copse of trees on the right. Cross another stile by a farm gate. You now have a copse and wall on your left.

4. In the top left-hand corner of the field enter another walled track for a few metres, before continuing in the same direction to enter another short walled track. {C} At

the end of this section of track bear right across and down the field aiming for a farm gate.

5. Cross the stile onto the Tissington Trail and turn right. {D}

6. Follow the trail for nearly 1 ¼ miles to a crossing of paths. Turn right up a long flight of steps to cross a stile. {E}

7. Keep straight on across the field aiming for a gate/gateway. Go through the gated stile. Bear very slightly left across the next field aiming for another gate/gateway. Go through another gated stile.

8. Bear left across the third field to go through a small gate leading to the road.{F}

9. Turn right then left by the butchers shop. At the next road junction turn left to retrace your outward route back to the car park.

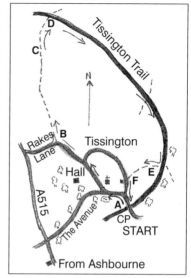

WALK 8
Wetton and Manifold Way

Wetton, Wetton Hill, Manifold Way, Beeston Tor, Carr Lane

Map: Explorer OL24 White Peak
Parking: Grid Ref SK109552
Distance: 5 miles
Approx. Time: 3 hours
Grade: 3★
Paths: Moorland and dale paths and surfaced tracks
Stiles: SS
Refreshments: The Royal Oak, Wetton

Picnic: Possibly instruction 11 as you reach the top of the climb!

Toilets: At the car park

Directions

From Ashbourne take the A515 Buxton road. In about 5 ½ miles turn left signed Alstonefield. Stay on this road into and through Alstonefield then follow the Wetton signs first down into Hope, where you turn right, still following the Wetton route. The road is very narrow and twisty. On reaching Wetton turn left at the car park and toilet sign.

Description

A walk of contrasts from the quiet stone built village of Wetton. The easy route between the high rounded Wetton Hills gives fine views of the Staffordshire White Peak before a peaceful stroll down the dale between the hills to join the busier, flat, surfaced Manifold Way. The return to Wetton gives you a chance to climb some quite steep hills with wonderful views before walking into Wetton.

Route Instructions

1. From the car park turn left down the road and at the T-junction turn left again to walk up through the village ignoring roads off to the right and passing The Royal Oak. Where the road bends left bear right up a wide surfaced lane. {A}

2. Follow this lane, ignoring the stile on the right, and shortly passing a reservoir installation on the right. {B} Go through the gate then through the squeeze stile ahead.

3. Follow the path up round the hill to go through another squeeze stile.

4. Keep straight on across the hillside. Soon you will see a barn down on the left and a stile in the fence at the bottom of the hill. Cross this stile and aim for the wall over on the left, to cross a stile in the field corner.

5. Keeping the wall close on your left continue down the field and at a wall corner turn left still following the line of the wall. {C} At the next fork of paths bear left, {D} with the wall on the left. As you approach a house ahead, bear off right to cross a footbridge and a stile.

6. Turn left below the house to go through a gate onto Access land. {E}

7. Follow the gradually descending dale path for about ¾ mile. Cross the stile by a gate at the bottom of the dale and keep straight on. {F}

8. At the junction with the Manifold Way keep straight on to cross a wide wooden bridge. (If you wish a light refreshment stop at Wetton Mill turn right for about ¼ mile)

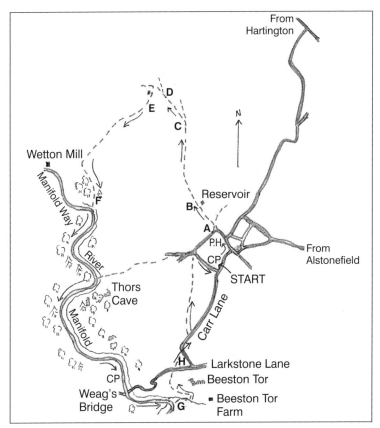

9. Walk along the flat Manifold Way to Weag's Bridge, 1 ¼ miles. After passing the car park cross the minor road by the bridge to take the left hand track.

10. Follow the track with the dry Manifold Valley still on the left. Walk passed the caravan site to cross a footbridge over the Hamps River. {G} Continue along the partly surfaced farm track towards Beeston Tor Farm. In a few metres and before reaching Beeston Tor Farm, turn left at a footpath sign to go through a gate.

11. Walk down a path and across the dry river bed, or if wet keep straight on to cross the stepping stones. Turn left to cross a stile onto "National Trust Beeston Tor" land. (Notice the magnificent limestone cliffs of Beeston Tor) Walk up the short steep bank to a footpath sign. Turn left up a wide fairly steep grass path by the gorse (wonderful

views). Cross a stile by a gate and turn right to follow a wall on the right and the line of an old wall on the left.

12. Cross a stile onto the minor road and bear right across Larkstone Lane to cross a stile. {H}

13. Bear right up the steep field to cross a stile onto Carr Lane. Turn left up the lane for about 300 metres then cross another stile on the left.

14. Bear right across the field to go through a squeeze stile to the right of a gate/gateway. Keep straight on across the next field. Cross a wall stile by the footpath post.

15. Bear slightly left to the top corner of the field. Go through the gate/ gateway.

16. Walk ahead to join a concrete farm track. Cross the farmyard via gate/gates. Walk down to the road and turn right.

17. At the T-junction turn left back to the car park.

WALK 9
Ashford-in-the-Water and Monsal Head

Ashford, Little Longstone, Monsal Head, Pennyunk Lane

Map: Explorer OL 24 White Peak
Parking: Grid Ref SK 195697
Distance: 4 miles
Approx. Time: 2 hours
Grade: 2
Paths: Field paths and tracks with a partly steep stepped path
Stiles: SS
Picnic: Instruction 10
Refreshments: The Aisseford Tea Rooms in Ashford and Packhorse Inn in Little Longstone

Directions

From Bakewell take the A6 Buxton road. In 1 ½ miles turn right at the A6020 Chesterfield and Sheffield sign. In a few metres turn left into Ashford village. Keep straight on passing the church. At the end of the road turn right up Fennel Street. Near the top of the street turn right to follow the car parking signs.

Description

This delightful walk across fields and along tracks will give you plenty of time to walk round the very pretty village of Ashford-in-the-Water and enjoy some refreshment. It is well worth a stop at Monsal Head where the views down to the viaduct and along the dale are very impressive.

Route Instructions

1. Leave the car park to walk back to Fennel Street and turn right up Vicarage Lane. At the top of the lane ignore Highfield Lane on the left and keep straight on for about another 120 metres.{A}

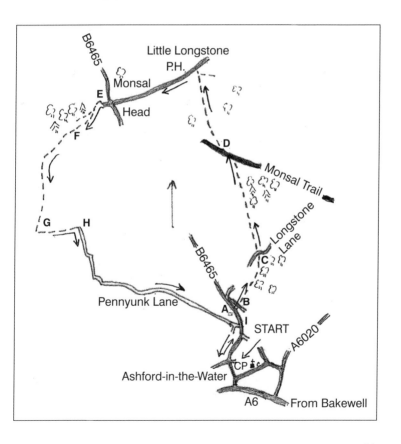

2. Cross a stile on the right and keep straight on across the field to go through a gate. Cross the road slightly left to enter a walled track {B} passing a barn and crossing a stile ahead.

3. Follow the wall on the right up the field and continue in the same direction passing through gates then a stile.

4. {C} Cross Longstone Lane and go over the stile. Bear very slightly left passing a stand of trees on the right. Go through a gated stile. Now keep straight on along a shallow valley crossing four stiles. At the wall ahead walk up the steps.

5. Cross the Monsal Trail diagonally left to go over the wall stile.{D}

6. Turn left down the field keeping the wall close on the left. Go through the gate. Keep straight on crossing two fields and going through two gates.

7. At the road in Little Longstone turn left passing The Packhorse Inn (a suitable half-way refreshment stop). Follow the road to Monsal Head (½ mile).

8. At the T-junction cross the B6465 by the Monsal Head Hotel and walk in front of Hobb's Café to go through the stile nearest to the café.{E}

9. Turn left, and almost immediately bear left signed Ashford. Follow the narrow partly stepped wooded path steeply uphill. Go through a gate and shortly you will have a wall on the left.

10. At the top of this path are two convenient seats with far reaching views where you can rest! {F}

11. Turn left to go through a small gate. Walk along a walled track, the middle part of which has lost the wall on the right. After about 500 metres and having gone through two gates and one stile you will pass a dew pond before going through a gate on the left. {G}

12. Follow a wall on the right down the field and cross the stile in the field corner. {H}

13. Follow the winding walled track of Pennyunk Lane for just over 1 mile.

14. {I} At the road junction near Highfields turn right to walk back into Ashford-in-the-Water.

WALK 10

Bakewell and Over Haddon

Bakewell Car Park, Haddon Hall, Over Haddon, Ditch Cliff, Bakewell

Map: Explorer OL 24 White Peak
Parking: Grid Ref SK 221687
Distance: 6 miles
Approx. Time: 3 ½ hours
Grade: 2
Paths: Riverside and field paths
Stiles: SS
Refreshments: Over Haddon and Bakewell

Directions

From Derby take the A6 to Bakewell. About a mile past the entrance to Haddon Hall and just before you get into Bakewell turn right. Follow the Agricultural Way to parking areas for the town centre, Agricultural Centre, and Bakewell Show.

Description

This is an easy walk following the River Wye to the entrance to Haddon Hall, then a gentle climb across open farmland up to Over Haddon. You will have a good view of Lathkill Dale where you can picnic. If you wish for more creature comforts then continue up to The Lathkill Hotel. After a mainly downhill walk you will return to the top end of Bakewell. A stroll through Bakewell will bring you back to the car park via the crossing of the Wye River, where the duck population is prolific.

Route Instructions

1. From the car park walk back down the Agricultural Way and where it bends right keep straight on. {A}

2. Follow the fence, trees and hedge close on the left crossing a stile and going through a small gate. After the gate turn sharp left over a footbridge and then turn right. {B} Veer away slightly from the hedge on your right. Cross two footbridges to the left of a small gate.

3. Follow the footpath sign keeping the hedge and stream close on the right. Go through a small gate and keep straight on signed "Bowling Green Fm". The River Wye is to your right.

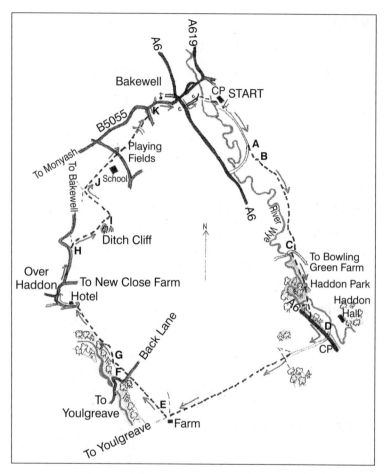

4. After about a mile from the start pass through a gate and turn right along the lane for about 30 metres. Turn left over a metal stile. {C}

5. Follow the riverside path through the wood and cross the rather impressive stone bridge before climbing the path to the A6.

6. Turn left down the road and just before Haddon Hall car park cross the busy A6. {D} Go through the gate to pass the car park on your left then through another gate.

7. Stay on the bridleway, with a wall on the right, as you climb the hill. Go through

a third gate. Continue in the same direction crossing three large fields, keeping the walls on the left and going through one gate and one stile to the left of a farm gate. (This is the Youlgreave route)

8. In the third field you will pass a farm near the field corner where you go through a small gate. {E}

9. Bear right and aim for the white building up ahead in Over Haddon. Cross a stile and continue in the same direction to cross a lane via two stiles. Keep straight on to go through a small gate.

10. {F} Follow the path above the River Lathkill until you reach a fence stile on the right. {G} Cross this stile and bear left up the field aiming for a waymarked post. Go through two small gates and continue uphill aiming to the right of The Lathkill Hotel.

11. Cross the stile to walk in front of the hotel. Take the right-hand fork uphill to join another road and continue ahead to the next road junction. Turn right along the Bakewell Road passing Manor Court. Leave the village and ignore the road to New Close Farm. In about ½ mile, at a left bend, leave the road to keep straight on through a stile by the footpath post. {H}

12. Walk down the steep hill to cross a gated stile. Turn right to walk towards and past the next footpath post. Follow the path as it gradually descends to the valley bottom, where you have a wall on the left. Continue to follow this wall until you reach a gated stile on the left. {I} Cross this stile and turn left.

13. Walk up the field, keeping a wall on the right, to cross the stile in the field corner. Keep straight on. You now have a wall on the left and soon lose the wall on the right. As you near the field corner turn right still keeping the field boundary close on the left.

14. {J} Cross the stile in the field corner and keep straight on to go through a gate.

15. Walk along the path by Lady Manners School. At the road junction keep straight on across it to follow the path by the tennis courts and playing fields. Go through a gate and on down first the tarmac path then the pavement before crossing the estate road and following a path between houses. This path soon widens out into a minor road. Where this road bends right keep straight on down steps to the road.

16. Turn left down the road. {K} At the T-junction, turn right down Monyash road. At the junction with the A6 turn right to cross the road at the pedestrian crossing and continue along the A6 to take the next left turn. Walk past the police station and where the road bends left bear off right to cross the paved area and the bridges over the Wye. This leads back to the car park.

WALK 11

Monsal Head and Monsal Dale

Monsal Head, the viaduct, Brushfield Hough, Monsal Dale, the weir, Monsal Head

Map: Explorer OL 24 White Peak

Parking: Grid Ref SK 185715

Distance: 3 ½ miles

Approx. Time: 2 hours

Grade: 3

Paths: Steep woodland paths, tracks and riverside paths

Stiles: S

Picnic: Monsal Dale and instruction 8

Refreshments: Monsal Head

Directions

From Bakewell take the A6 Buxton road. In 1 ½ miles turn right on the A6020 then left into Ashford-in-the-Water on the B6465 which almost immediately turns right signed Monsal Head. Follow this road for about 1 ¼ miles. Turn left into Monsal Head Car Park.

Description

A short varied walk where you will be rewarded with wonderful views after a climb up from the viaduct. A delightful but steep woodland path takes you down into the wide Monsal Dale with towering woodlands on both sides. This easy riverside walk will refresh you for the climb back up to Monsal Head.

Route Instructions

1. From the car park walk up the passageway between the hotel and the Stable Bar. Turn left and opposite the cafe go through the wider wall gap. Turn right down the stone steps. In a few yards turn left to continue down a path signed "Viaduct & Monsal Trail". {A}

2. Turn right across the viaduct and just past the end turn left through the first small gate to follow the Brushfield route.

3. Walk up the steep rocky path. At a bridleway sign on the right continue up the stony and rocky track. At the top pass through a gate. {B} If you divert a few metres to the left you will have wonderful views. Return to the track for another half mile.

4. Pass through a stile by a gate then follow the wall close on the left to cross another

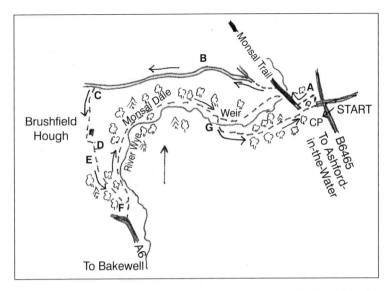

stile by a gate. In a few metres and past a wide wall gap, cross a wall stile on the right. {C} (not easily seen, if you reach the field corner you have passed it!)

5. Having crossed the stile keep straight on across the field to go through a gate/gateway by the waymarked post.

6. Walk down Brushfield Hough Farm drive passing the farm buildings. Just before the last building on the left turn left through the gate/gateway. {D} Walk across the yard to turn right through another gate then the gateway.

7. Bear left to join a track by a footpath post and turn right. Where the track bends right veer left off the track to cross a wall stile. {E}

8. Turn right (a good picnic spot), to follow a grass path down through the scrub. Soon the path bears round to the left and becomes more definite.

9. Descend the steep wooded hillside taking care especially if the path is wet. As you near the bottom of the hill the path becomes stepped. At a fork of paths take the right fork down to the Monsal Dale path.

10. {F} Turn left to walk along Monsal Dale. In about 15 to 20 minutes the dale opens out. Fork right down to a footbridge below the weir.

11. {G} Cross the footbridge and turn left.

12. Walk through the woods passing the weir and going through a gate. Continue uphill for about ½ mile back to Monsal Head.

WALK 12

Monsal Head and Rowland

Monsal Head, Great Longstone, Rowland, Monsal Trail, Little Longstone, Monsal Head

Map: Explorer OL 24 White Peak
Parking: Grid Ref SK 185715
Distance: 5 miles
Approx. Time: 2 ½ hours
Grade: 1
Paths: Field paths, minor road and trail
Stiles: SSS
Refreshments: Great and Little Longstone

Directions

See Walk 11

Description

On this easy walk you can again marvel at the wonderful views from Monsal Head. There are no steep climbs as you stroll across fields and along Monsal Trail visiting three villages.

Route Instructions

1. From the car park walk back to the entrance and turn left along the B6465 for a few metres, {A} then turn right to follow the road into Little Longstone. Just past The Packhorse Inn and opposite "Little Longstone Barns" turn right.

2. Cross the left-hand wall stile by the footpath post, signed "Great Longstone". {B} Keep straight on up the hill. As you near the top of the hill you will see a small fence enclosure on the right. Continue aiming for a fence stile ahead.

3. {C} Cross the stile to walk along a short path to go through a small waymarked gate.

4. Walk almost diagonally across the next field aiming for a stile in the wall ahead and passing a single tree over to the right.

5. Cross a stile then the track to go through a small gate. Keep straight on for a few metres to go through another gate.

6. Continue in the same direction across the middle of the next field. Go through a small gate in the wall ahead. Follow the field boundary on the left to cross a stile.

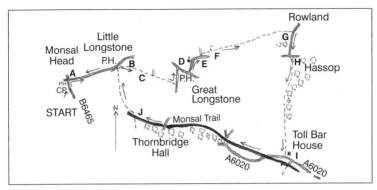

7. On reaching the village road in Great Longstone turn left. {D}

8. Walk down the road to the T-junction in Great Longstone. Turn right to walk through the village.

9. Opposite The White Lion turn left to walk up Church Lane.

10. Pass the church and about 100 metres from the right-hand bend in the road turn left into a track. {E} Almost immediately turn right through a stile.

11. Bear left across the field corner to go through a stile. Turn right along a track for about 100 metres and where it bends left keep straight on down the bank to cross a stile. {F}

12. Continue ahead in a north easterly direction, crossing five undulating fields, five stiles, one gate and three tracks.

13. Follow a wall on the right to go through a stile and pass a barn on the left. Keep straight on crossing two more fields and stiles to reach the road in Rowland. {G}

14. Turn right to walk down the road junction. Cross the road diagonally left to the high wall round Hassop. {H}

15. Follow the track for about 200 metres then cross a stile on the right. Now follow the high wall close on your left. Cross three stiles and at the wall corner bear off right down the field passing the waymarked post and aiming to the right of the Toll Bar House. {I} Cross the stile onto the A6020.

16. Turn left and opposite the Toll Bar House turn right through the gate. Keep straight on to go through the gap onto the Monsal Trail.

17. Turn right to follow the trail for just over 1 mile to where the trail leaves the track to cross a stone stile on the right. {J}

18. Follow a wall close on the left down the field to go through a gate. Cross two fields and gates to reach the road in Little Longstone.

19. Turn left to retrace your outward route back to Monsal Head.

WALK 13

Calton Lees and Rowsley

Calton Lees Car Park, Calton Lees Hamlet, Calton Plantations, Bouns Corner, Rowsley, Derwent Valley Heritage Way, Calton Lees

Map: Explorer OL 24 White Peak
Parking: Grid Ref SK 258686
Distance: 5 miles
Approx. Time: 2 ½ hours
Grade: 2
Paths: Tracks, field and woodland paths
Stiles: S
Refreshments: Rowsley and Chatsworth Garden Centre
Toilets: Chatsworth Garden Centre

Directions

From Baslow take the Bakewell road A619 and where it turns right keep straight on along the B6012 Chatsworth road driving through the park. Immediately after crossing the second cattle grid turn right into the car park.

Description

A pleasant and varied walk, most of the uphill climb is at the start of the walk. The views over Chatsworth and down the Derwent Valley are wonderful and far reaching. May is a good time to follow this route when the bridleway through the woods may be drier and the bluebells will be in bloom. In Instruction 6 be aware of the many sheep tracks which could be mistaken for the route.

Route Instructions

1. From the car park walk towards the Garden Centre then continue along the minor road to Calton Lees.

2. {A} Go through the middle of the three gates to walk up the track to Calton Houses (about 15 to 20 minutes).

3. Go through the gate to walk past Calton Barns and Calton House. At the end of the track go through another farm gate and turn left. {B}

4. Follow the wall and the bluebell wood on the left. At a waymarked post turn left down a short walled track to cross a stile. {C}

5. Continue along the track with a wall on the left for a few metres before branching off right, still on a farm track. In a few metres the track (now a path) branches off left. Aim for the waymarked post ahead.

6. Cross a gully in the field, where there are water troughs, and aim uphill towards a conifer wood. Soon you will see a ladder stile ahead.

7. {D} Cross the stile to continue ahead to follow the bridleway through the wood. In about 100 metres turn left, still on the bridleway, to walk through a more open woodland area. Before reaching a gate the bridleway branches right by a short way-marked post. Continue to follow the winding route which eventually goes through a gateway.([A possible picnic area) {E}

8. Turn left to follow a wall on the left. Shortly the bridleway bears off right away from the wall to descend on a clear route down through the wood.

9. {F} At a T-junction of tracks turn left. In about 100 metres and just before a gate turn right. Continue to descend through and out of the wood.

10. At a junction of four tracks pass a gate on the left to turn left by the metal boom.

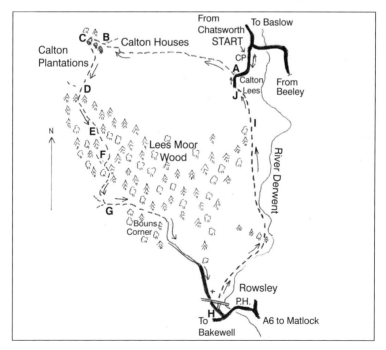

11. {G} Walk up the walled track. From here there are wonderful views over to your right. At the top of the hill keep straight on down through the open woodland. After about 450 metres pass by another metal boom to turn right.

12. Continue down the track which leads eventually into Rowsley.

13. Walk through the village passing the church on the left. {H} At Home Farm turn left to follow the Calton Lees and Chatsworth route.

14. Walk under the bridge via a gate. Follow the wide track with the river over to the right.

15. Where the track ends keep straight on across the field with a wall on the left. Cross a stile by a gate to follow a well used path through trees then over another stile.

16. Aim for a fence corner then follow the fence on your right for a few metres before veering away from it and the river. Aim now for a gateway ahead.

17. Go through the gateway and keep straight on to cross a wall stile to the left of another gate/gateway.

18. Bear slightly left to follow a wall on the left uphill. Near the top of the hill cross a ladder stile by a gate. {I}

19. Turn right to keep a wall close on the right. Walk above Calton Lees. {J} Cross a stile on the right to walk down the minor road in Calton Lees.

20. At the road junction turn right to retrace your outward route back to the car park.

WALK 14

Chatsworth and Edensor

Chatsworth House Car Park, Edensor, Calton Pastures, New Piece Wood, Edensor

Map: Explorer OL 24 White Peak
Parking: Grid Ref SK 259704
Distance: 5 miles
Approx. Time: 2 ½ to 3 hours
Grade: 2
Paths: Estate paths, tracks and a minor road
Stiles: S
Refreshments: Chatsworth Restaurant and Edensor Tea Rooms

Directions

From Baslow take the B6012. Ignore all side roads to drive into Chatsworth Park. Follow the signs to Chatsworth House then follow the signs to car parking areas. These will vary according to the demand for parking space. Pay at the entrance kiosk.

Description

No walk book is complete without a Chatsworth walk! There are four walks in this area in our other books. This walk takes you to the pretty village of Edensor on the outward route and again before you return to the car park. The tea rooms at the village store offer a refreshing cup of tea or coffee. After a steady climb on a track from Edensor and then up a minor road you will walk across Calton Pasture where there are wide extensive views.

Route Instructions

1. From the car park walk back to the bridge and cross it. {A}

2. {B} Walk up the path ahead, through the trees, to the B6012.

3. Cross the road to enter the village of Edensor. Walk through this pretty village, keeping the church on the left, then on up the track for about ¾ mile.

4. {C} Turn left up a minor road. After about ½ mile at the corner of a wood and a bend in the road turn left up a track. {D}

5. Follow this track and go through a gate. At a fork bear right keeping the Moatless Plantation copse on the left. Shortly you will bear right by a waymarked post. Walk down the hill towards a pond.

6. {E} At a crossing of paths go through a small gate by the pond. Keep straight on with

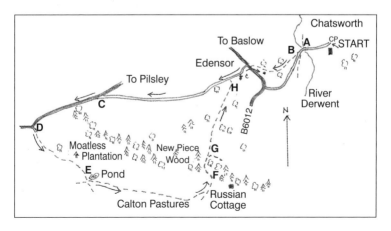

a fence on your left. In about 350 metres go through a small gate and bear right downhill with a fence on your right. Cross a stile and continue ahead. Eventually you will see Russian Cottage, a black and white building at the edge of a wood. At a crossing of paths and before reaching the cottage turn left. Enter New Piece Wood via a farm gate. {F}

7. Walk through the wood on a wide track. Cross a high wall stile by the gate.

8. Walk down the field to a waymarked post {G} then on down following the yellow waymarked arrows to pass a fenced copse over on the right. Continue downhill under the trees to pass another fenced copse also on the right. Where the fence bends round to the right keep straight on.

9. Aim for the spire of Edensor church ahead. As you near the village keep the church over to your right and pass a waymarked post on the left.

10. {H} To enter the village climb the steps ahead to go through the metal gate then on down steps into the village.

11. Turn right to retrace your outward route.

(If you wish to visit the tea rooms and toilet turn right, by the church, just before you leave the village. The toilets are in the courtyard past the shop and tearoom.)

WALK 15
White Edge and Froggatt Edge

Curbar Gap Car Park, White Edge, The Grouse Inn, Froggatt Edge, Curbar Edge

Map: Explorer OL 24 White Peak
Parking: Grid Ref SK 262747
Distance: 6 miles
Approx. Time: 3 hours
Grade: 2
Paths: Moorland
Stiles: S
Refreshments: The Grouse Inn
Picnic: Froggatt and Curbar Edges

Directions

From Baslow take the A623 Stockport and Manchester road. In 1 ½ miles turn right to Curbar and in a few metres bear off right up Curbar Lane signed "Curbar Village".

Follow this steep uphill road for about a mile, passing lay-bys on the left. At the top of the hill turn left into the pay and display car park.

Description

This has always been a favourite walk of ours. The far reaching views from all the edges can be enjoyed with only one short climb at the start of the route. The paths are easy to follow with just a few places were you will climb the huge gritstone rocks. These mainly flat rocks are ideal picnic sites. Froggatt and Curbar Edges are very popular with both walkers and rock climbers.

Route Instructions

1. Leave the car park with the road on your right, crossing the entrance. Go through the gate to enter the "Eastern Moors Estate".

2. Keep straight on for about 100 metres to a wall corner on the left and at this point leave the wall to keep straight on. (do NOT bear round to the left) {A}

3. Continue down the moorland track aiming for the steep slope ahead. Cross a wooden bridge to climb the only steep slope on the walk.

4. {B }Turn sharp left at the wall corner signed "White Edge". Shortly bear right away from the wall up onto the moors.

5. Follow the concessionary path along White Edge for about 2

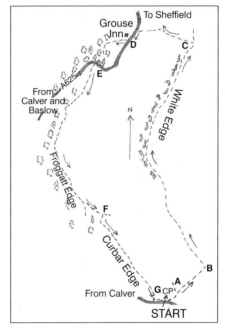

miles. In about 45 minutes you will pass through a wide walled gap.

6. {C} Turn left down the moorland keeping a wall on the left. As you go down the hill over the gritstone rocks you leave the wall and bear off right. In a few metres turn left down through the woods. Go through a gate on the left walk diagonally aiming for The Grouse Inn via a gate.

7. Turn left down the road and just past The Grouse Inn turn right over a stile. {D}

8. Walk down three fields passing through a gate then aiming for a small gate in the wall ahead. Go through this small gate and turn left.

9. Follow the path through the woods passing a car park on your left. Walk downhill to cross a stream then on up a steep bank to the road.

10. Turn right then cross the busy road to go through a gateway by the farm gate. {E}

11. Walk up the wide track to enter the birch wood. Go through a small gate and continue along Froggatt Edge. In about a mile from the road ignore a waymarked post on the right to continue along the wide main route of Curbar Edge. Shortly the path divides, at this point take the right fork {F} up to the rocks ahead.

12. After about 2 miles from the road leave the edges via a small gate. {G} Keep straight on across a small embankment. Follow the path with the wall on the left back to the car park.

WALK 16
Errwood Reservoir

Errwood Reservoir Car Park, Bunsal Cob, Wild Moor, Goyt Valley

Map: Explorer OL24 White Peak
Parking: SK 013747
Distance: 4 ½ miles
Approx. Time: 2 ½ to 3 hours
Grade: 2 (or 2* for the 2b route)
Paths: Moorland paths and tracks and reservoir road
Stiles: none!
Picnic: Errwood Reservoir area
Toilets: Near Bunsal Cob (if open)

Directions

From the centre of Buxton take the A5004 Whaley Bridge road and in 2 ¼ miles take the first turn left after leaving Buxton. Follow Goyt's Lane for 1 ½ miles down to the reservoirs. Just after crossing between them turn left. Ignore the first car park entrance to drive down the reservoir road for about ¾ mile. Turn right into the second car park.

Description

While following paths and tracks across the moorland above the reservoir you will have far reaching wonderful views on a clear day. There are some stretches that can be rather boggy, particularly at instruction 8. The valley and reservoir roads and paths are very pretty and offer a number of picnic spots. Please note, if you follow this route on a Sunday or Bank Holiday the road by the reservoir is closed to vehicles between 1st May and 30th September. You will need to park at the first reservoir car park and start the walk at instruction 2. At instruction 2 you have a choice either (2a) to follow the easier road route to instruction (6) or (2b) the more strenuous and interesting paths below the dam and round Bunsal Cob.

Route Instructions

1. Leave the second car park to walk back along the road, passing the first car park.{A}

2. (2a) Turn right down the road and across the dam to continue up and round Bunsal

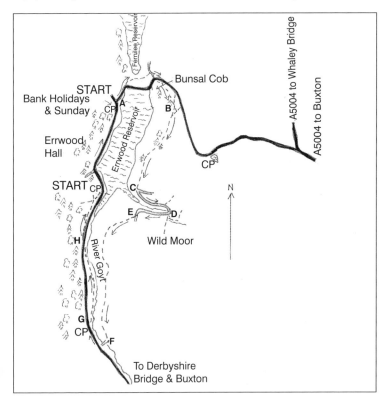

Cob. In about ½ mile from the first car park and at a small layby on the right turn right by the Access Land notice. Follow the path, which soon has a wood on the right. Join the (2b) route at the end of instruction 5. {B}

(2b) In a few metres, at the road junction, take the Fernilee path ignoring the dam road. Walk down to and through the small gate. At a fence corner turn right down the steep grass slope and soon you will have a fence on the right. Just before a farm gate and a small gate turn right to follow the Bunsal and Fernilee circular path. Take care down the short path to the path below the dam.

3. Pass the end of the Fernilee Reservoir on your left. Go through a small gate and turn right up the road. Part way up the hill branch off left to continue up the grassy bank to the road.

4. Walk up the road and just before the toilets and the top end of the small car park on the left turn right to leave the road. There is no sign at this point and the path may be somewhat obscured in the summer.

5. Follow a path uphill with a fence and Bunsal Cob on the right. Soon the path veers off left up over the grassy moorland before dropping down steeply to walk through a narrow belt of conifers. A short gentle hill takes you up to a T-junction of paths where you turn right. {B}

6. In a few metres cross a broken wall on the left to continue in the same direction and join another path. Walk towards and through a wooded area.

7. Follow a wall on the left which you will soon lose as you cross moorland and broken walls.

8. In about ¾ mile from Bunsal Cob you will come to a junction of paths and a bench over looking the reservoir. (a good coffee stop!) {C} Take the second path on the left, by the footpath sign, to follow a wide path with the reservoir inlet down on the right.

9. In about ¼ mile cross a footbridge on the right {D} to follow the Goyt's Clough Quarry sign. Stay on the track for just over ¼ mile, passing through a gate and having a wall on the right for the last few metres, until you reach a sign post. {E} Leave the track to turn right down a narrow path with a wall on the right.

10. Cross a footbridge and go on up the slope still with the wall on the right for another 200 metres. Pass through a wall gap and continue in the same direction with the wall now up on the left. As you cross the moorland the bracken gives way to a more open, rather boggy area with some stretches crossed via duck boards.

11. In just over ½ mile from the footbridge (inst. 8) you will see the car park at Goyt's Clough Quarry and the small stone packhorse bridge down to the right.

12. Walk down to and across the bridge then on up to the road {F} and turn right

along the road.

13. About 50 metres past the car park leave the road by a small layby to follow the "Riverside Path". {G}

14. Walk down the steep, winding and partly stepped path to the River Goyt. Cross the footbridge to follow the river on your right. Along this very pleasant undulating woodland path you will cross 4 footbridges in all before reaching the road via a small gate.

15. Cross the road diagonally right to go up 3 steps adjacent to a metal gate. {H}

16. Walk along a wide undulating track for about ½ mile. At a crossing of tracks and paths turn right through a gateway.

17. Follow a path down to the car park and picnic benches.

WALK 17

Hollinsclough and Chrome Hill

Hollinsclough, Leycote, Booth Farm, Chrome Hill, Stannery, Hollinsclough

Map: Explorer OS 24

Parking: Where safe in Hollinsclough

Distance: 4 ½ miles.

Approx. Time: 3 ½ hours

Grade: 3★

Paths: Stony tracks, steep path with some rock climbing and a rather wet area above the River Dove

Stiles: S

Refreshments: On a Sunday tea and cakes in Hollinsclough village

Picnic: The top of Chrome Hill! Or at Instruction 13 {F}

Directions

From Buxton take the A515 Ashbourne road. In about 3 ½ miles at Brierlow Bar turn right to follow the B5053 Longnor road. Drive through Glutton and over Glutton Bridge. In just over ½ mile turn sharp right onto a minor road for just over 1 mile into Hollinsclough.

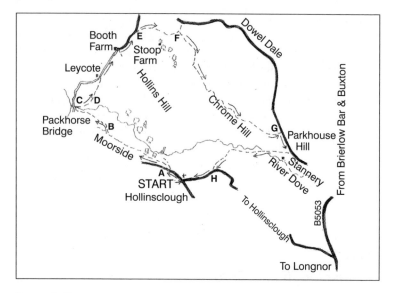

Description

This is a fascinating area of steep rocky limestone ridges which are the remains of coral reefs formed more than 320 million years ago. These hills tower above the grassy farmland meadows and open moorland, across which are numerous paths and tracks. It is like a miniature Lake District! To enjoy this walk you need to be fit and not afraid of heights or a little rock climbing. It is the most challenging walk in the book. Boots are a must even in dry weather because the path in instruction 2 is crossed by a number of springs.

If you do not wish to climb Chrome Hill keep straight on over the stile by the cattle grid at {F} instruction 13 to walk along the track where you join a minor road which leads down Dowel Dale. Rejoin the route at Instruction 17.

Route Instructions

1. From the centre of the village walk up the road passing the Methodist Chapel on the right and the Chapel Hall on the left. In about 200 metres turn right at a footpath post to go through a small gate.

2. In about 75 metres take the left hand higher path {A} to climb and contour the hillside. Cross a stile in the open woodland. You will be following an intermittent broken wall. (This area can be quite muddy and you will need to find the best route) Eventually you will see a wide ascending grass and shale track, aim for this track.

3. On reaching the track turn right down a grassy track to pass a stone barn close on your left. {B} Soon you will see a waymarked post then another post under the large holly bush further along. The upper stretch of the River Dove is down to your right.

4. Cross a small stream via a stone slab on your right, then cross a stile. Cross the next larger stream via the stones before crossing the old packhorse bridge.

5. Immediately after crossing the bridge go through a gated stile on the right. {C}

6. Pass a barn on your left and aim slightly left to go through the smaller wall gap just below the gorse bushes.

7. Climb the hillside to pass through another wall gap.

8. Contour the hillside keeping the bushes and trees fairly close on the left. Cross a broken wall by a gorse bush and keep straight on. Go through a gated stile above a large holly bush. {D}

9. Follow a wall on the right. Soon you will see Leycote Farm ahead. Go through a small gate to the left and adjacent to a farm gate.

10. Walk through the farmyard to go through another farm gate. Turn right.

11. Follow the track to Booth Farm where you join a minor road.

12. Continue along the road for about 300 metres and where it starts to climb the hillside cross a stile on the right by a cattle grid. {E}

13. Follow the track to cross another stile. Keep straight on and up the field aiming for the footpath posts ahead. At the third post turn right to follow the concessionary path to Chrome Hill. {F}

14. Follow the wall on the left to go through two gates. After crossing a broken wall bear right to pass a waymarked post then follow a fence steeply downhill. Cross the fence stile on the left.

15. Stay on the low level grassy path below the hill to go through a gate. Turn left to start your climb. The route meanders steeply up and around the hill where there is some rock scrambling.

16. Eventually you are rewarded with magnificent views.

17. The descent is down a very steep grass path. Cross a stile then on across a narrow rocky ridge aiming for the high peaks of Parkhouse Hill. At the bottom of Chrome Hill, aim for the minor road and a stile. {G}

18. Cross the stile and turn right along the minor road. At the footpath post turn right again down the track to go through the Stannery Farm gate. Cross the cattle grid to keep straight on following the waymarked post. Cross the footbridge by the ford. Continue ahead along the track. At a T-junction turn left to Hollinsclough

19. {H} At the road junction turn right back to Hollinsclough.

WALK 18

Three Shire Heads and the Dane Valley

Gradbach Car Park, Dane Valley, Three Shire Heads, Cut-thorn Hill, A54, Crag Hall, Firs Farm, Heild End Farm, Goosetree, Y.H.A. Gradbach

Map: Explorer OL24 White Peak
Parking: SJ 998663 at Gradbach
Distance: 6 miles
Approx. Time: 4 hours
Grade: 3
Paths: Valley and moorland paths and tracks
Stiles: SS
Refreshments: Picnic at Three Shire Heads

Directions

From Leek take the A53 Buxton road. In 5 ½ miles turn left signed Gradbach. Follow this road for nearly 2 ½ miles ignoring all side roads, see map. At a T-junction turn left for 150 metres then turn left signed Scout Camp and Y.H.A. Follow this minor road to turn right into the car park.

Description

From the car park to Three Shire Heads you will be in the Staffordshire Peak following the Dane Valley. At the very picturesque Three Shire Heads you will cross the bridge where you will be in Derbyshire for a few steps before crossing into Cheshire where you stay until you reach the car park. If the weather is kind to you this is a really lovely walk even when somewhat wet under foot.

Route Instructions

1. From the car park take the waymarked path at the eastern end of the car park (ie furthest away from the entrance). Follow the path for about 100 metres, with the River Dane on the left. Go through a stile and immediately turn left over a footbridge.

2. Turn right across the meadow still following the river. In a few metres, after passing under the trees, bear right to cross a gated stile onto the road. Walk up the road round a bend for about 75 metres then turn left through a gate near the cottage. Bear right uphill to go through another a gate. {A}

3. Walk up the field to and through a gate passing a derelict building over to the left. Continue up the next four fields keeping a wall on the left and passing through gates,

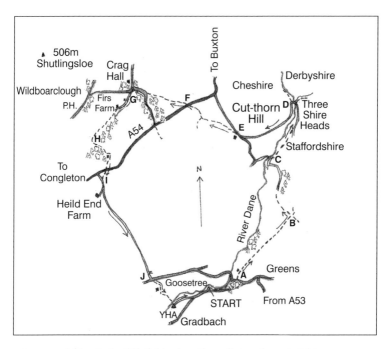

gateways and stiles. In the fifth field, where the wall stops, keep straight on.

4. Cross a stile by a gateway and continue ahead across a reedy area towards a small gate in the wall ahead, just before this gate turn left along an old grass track. {B} Cross a stile by a gate.

5. Keep straight on following the grass track as it winds round the hillside. When you meet a shale track, bear left onto it. Follow this track as it meanders down the hillside to pass a dilapidated barn on your left. Here the track turns left downhill to join another track. Turn right, keeping the river on the left and at a footbridge turn right again. {C}

6. Walk up the stony path still keeping the river on the left and in about 350 metres you will have a wall on the left. Continue along the well defined path above the River Dane passing through one gate until you reach Three Shire Heads and the bridge across the river. This is a favourite and lovely picnic stop about 2 miles from the car park at Gradbach.

7. Turn left over the bridge then left again. {D} Follow the stony track up and around

Cut-thorn Hill for nearly 1 mile. On reaching a minor road via a gate turn right and almost immediately cross a stile on the left by the house. {E}

8. Follow a wall on the left which shortly will veer away to the left. Keep straight on across the open moorland aiming for the flat top hill of Shutlingsloe in the distance. As you near a farm gate the route veers left up to a broken wall. Cross this wall and then a fence stile to keep straight on still aiming for Shutlingsloe. Go through a small gate.

9. Cross the busy A54 to go over a stile. {F}

10. Keep straight on still aiming for Shutlingsloe and following the partly duck boarded path across the reedy moors. Go through a farm gate and pass a small stone barn. Soon you will have a wall on the right as you descend to the conifer wood.

11. Go through a gate and on down the stony track to the road. Turn right down the road to the tree covered triangle. Stay on the left to pass the triangle and Crag Hall up to the right.

12. At the bottom of the triangle turn left through a gateway to walk up the track {G} going through another gate/gate-way to walk behind the house. Continue uphill on the track to go through another gate. Walk past Firs Farm via two gates.

13. Keep straight on following the wall and wood close on the left. Pass the waymarked post to enter a track. (The start of this track is very muddy!)

14. At the top of the track cross the wall stile {H} and keep straight on following first a wall then the wood close on the right before veering off left down to and through a gateway.

15. Follow the wall on the left to go through a gateway on the left. Keep straight on up the hill to walk behind the barn then continue in the same direction with a wall on the right for a short way. Gradually bear right uphill to cross a stile by a footpath post to the left of a farm gate.

16. Cross the road diagonally right to cross the fence stile. Walk up the steep path to join a surfaced track. {I}

17. Follow this track for about 100 metres then bear off left up a stony track, ignoring the drive to Heild End Farm.

18. Stay on the track for about a mile. You will pass through five gates and at the fifth one ignore the track on the left to keep straight on down to the road. {J}

19. Cross the minor road to walk down the partly surfaced track for about 150 metres and at the bend cross a stile on the left to follow a concessionary path close to the wall on your right. Turn left at the field corner to follow a wall on your right. In a few metres turn right through the wall gap.

20. Bear left then turn right down a steep grassy and rocky path aiming for the Y.H.A.

Cross the footbridge over the River Dane then walk in front of the hostel (once a mill). At the end of the building is a café open at weekends only.

21. {K} Turn left at the road junction to walk uphill. Follow this road back to the car park ignoring side roads.

WALK 19

Carsington Village and Hopton

Carsington Village, Carsington Pasture, Brassington Village, Pennine Bridleway (High Peak Trail), Old Knoll and Kings Chair, Hopton , Carsington Village

Map: Explorer OL 24 White Peak
Parking: In Carsington Village
Start of walk: Grid Ref SK251533
Distance: 5 ½ miles
Approx. Time: 3 hours
Grade: 2
Paths: Field paths, trail and minor road
Stiles: SSS
Refreshments: Carsington, Brassington and at the Reservoir Visitor Centre

Directions

From the Visitor Centre at Carsington Reservoir return to the B5035 and turn right. Pass the Knockerdown Inn and in about 1 ¼ miles turn left to Carsington Village. There is no official car park, so please park wherever safe. The walk starts at the bend in the road just as you enter the village.

Description

This is a varied and pleasant walk in one of the more gentle areas outside the Peak Park. The first part crosses open pasture land with wide views before you reach the hillside village of Brassington, once a lead mining and farming village. The district around is said to be haunted! Along the Pennine Bridle Way are many examples of old and new quarry sites. If you follow this route in February to early March you will be rewarded with wonderful displays of snowdrops at Hopton Hall.

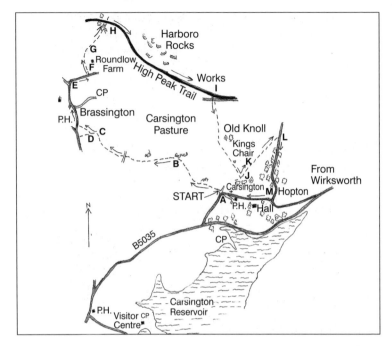

Route Instructions

1. From wherever you park walk back to the bend (see map). {A} Walk up the lane away from the village and in a north-west direction. (Do not take the path up between the houses)

2. {A} Cross a stile by a gate and continue ahead round the hillside. You will pass under power lines and have the hillside boundary on the left.

3. Cross a stile by two gates and keep straight on up through a small gully before continuing across higher ground. Aim for the old stones of a squeeze stile then go through it and turn right. {B}

4. Go through a broken wall gap ahead and on down the hill to cross a stile. Aim to the left of a ruined barn to cross a track via two stiles.

5. Keep straight on up the hill aiming for the mining humps. Follow the footpath arrow. Soon the path bends right through the humps then on down towards Brassington. Cross a squeeze stile.

6. Follow a wall on the left before crossing a stile on the left. {C}

7. About halfway down the steep field cross a stile in the wall on your right. {D} Walk across the next field to cross another stile. Bear left to cross a stepped gated stile in the field corner. Walk through the farmyard to the road where you turn right.

8. Walk up through Brassington, ignoring all side roads. About 300 metres after the last house turn right signed HOBEN. {E}

9. Follow the road for 300 metres then turn left up Roundlow Farm drive. {F} Pass the bungalow and at the farm turn right to follow the white arrows on the barn. Go through gated stile.

10. Walk diagonally left up the field passing close to two wall corners and walking towards the wall over on the left. Bear round to the right to keep the wall close on your left and pass a small rock outcrop and a stand of trees on the right. {G}

11. Cross a stile on the left just before a farm gate. Walk down the next two fields keeping the walls on the right and going through a gateway.

12. Walk through a small copse via two stiles, to reach the trail. {H}

13. Turn right along the Pennine Bridleway to follow the Middleton Top route. In a mile and having passed the brick works and a path to Brassington, leave the trail by the "Caution Vehicles Crossing" notice.

14. {I} Cross a low stile and follow a wall close on the left. Cross a road via two stiles.

15. Keep straight on down then up Carsington Pastures with a wall close on the left. Walk through a hummocky area of Old Knoll, still with the wall and a fence on the left and passing a waymarked post. Aim for the wood ahead. Notice the rocks on the left, this is the King's Chair.

16. {J} Cross the stile in the corner near the wood and by the footpath post.

17. Follow the wood on the right for about 100 metres and where it bends off right keep straight on. {K} Walk through a small outcrop of rocks (picnic), then on down a short steep bank to go through a gateway. Aim downhill for a fence corner then on uphill aiming for a gateway slightly to the right. Cross the stile by this gateway and pass a field corner. Aim for the road and the gateway in the field corner.

18. {L} Turn right to follow the minor road, for just over ½ mile, through the woods. {M} Turn right at the road junction to walk back to Carsington passing Hopton Hall.

WALK 20

Hartington and Beresford Dale

Hartington, Lower Hurst Farm, Beresford Dale, Hartington

Map: Explorer OL24 White Peak
Parking: Hartington Grid Ref SK128604
Distance: 3 ½ miles
Approx. Time: 2 hours
Grade: 1
Paths: Field and dale paths
Stiles: SS
Refreshments: Charles Cotton Hotel also inns and tea rooms in Hartington
Toilets: In Hartington

Direction

Hartington is just over 2 miles down the B5054 off the A515 Ashbourne to Buxton road about 10 miles north of Ashbourne. There is a small free parking area in the centre of the village and a pay and display car park a few metres down the Hulme End to Warslow road. (B5054)

Description

Starting from one of the most typical and often visited Derbyshire villages at Hartington, this walk provides you with a good amount of exercise initially across undulating fields then down the limestone dales. Beresford Dale is a delight all the year round.

Route Instructions

1. From whichever car park you use return to The Charles Cotton Hotel. With the hotel on your right walk up the B5054 Warslow road for a few metres and just before the Pottery on the left, turn right at the end of a wall in front of a row of stone houses. {A}

2. Follow the wall and house wall to pass through a stone squeeze stile. Continue along a very narrow path between the buildings, a fence and a wall passing through gates. Follow a wall close on the left round a small paddock to cross a stile in the paddock corner.

3. Keep straight on across the next five fields and stiles maintaining a south-westerly direction. In the fourth and fifth fields aim for a cottage and the road.

4. After the fifth stile walk to the B5054 {B} and turn right. Walk up the road for about

500 metres, passing into Staffordshire. Pass Raikes Farm on the right and the drive to Lower Hurst Farm on the left.

5. Just past the "Little Raikes Footpath" sign and the cottage on the left, turn left at the next footpath sign. {C} Cross the stile and descend the field keeping a wall and fence on the left.

6. Go through a gate and across a footbridge to walk straight on up the next field going through a small gate.

7. Keep straight on to Lower Hurst Farm. {D}

8. Cross a stile and follow the fence close on the right below the farm. Cross two more stiles and a small paddock to go through a squeeze stile.

9. {E} Turn left to cross a cattle grid then turn right to follow the wood close on the right.

10. Go through three small gates then over a small footbridge and a stile.

11. Keep straight on across a reedy field, soon you will have a wood on the left. Cross another footbridge and stile.

12. Keep straight on to go through a gate and stile to reach Beresford Lane. {F}

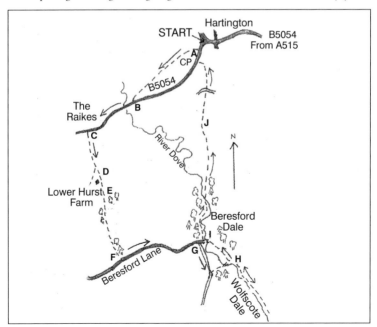

13. Turn left down the lane, for nearly ½ mile. Before you reach the river you have a choice: **Either** turn right through a gate {G} to walk up a track.

14. Go through another gate then turn sharp left through a third gate.

15. Walk down to the River Dove and cross it via a gated footbridge.

16. {H} Here you can turn right through a stile to walk down the magnificent Wolfscote Dale for as far as you wish (for a picnic!) then return to go back through the stile and keep straight on across the water meadows. Turn left across the footbridge then turn right along Beresford Dale. **Or** keep straight on down Beresford Lane to the river where you turn left (not across the footbridge).

17. {I} Walk along Beresford Dale keeping the river on your right. Cross the footbridge and follow a path which soon climbs up away from the river. Go through a gated stile.

18. Walk up the hill, bearing very slightly right. Pass three waymarked posts then turn down left towards a gate/gateway passing another waymarked post. Go through the gateway and keep straight on to go through another gateway.

19. {J} Turn right uphill then left by another waymarked post. Cross a track via two gates.

20. Follow a shale path with the wall then houses on the left to go through a gate and down steps by the toilets to reach the road into Hartington. Turn right to the village centre or left to the car park.

WALK 21

Hartington and Biggin Dale

Hartington Car Park, Hall Bank, YHA, Highfield Lane, Dale End, Biggin Dale, Reynards Lane, Hartington

Map: Explorer OL24 White Peak
Parking: SK 128604
Distance: 3 miles
Approx. Time: 1 ½ hours
Grade: 1
Paths: Tracks and minor roads with one short dale path and a short climb
Stiles: S
Refreshments: Hotel, inns and tea rooms in Hartington

Directions

Hartington is just over 2 miles on the B5054 from the A515. In the village there is a small parking area by the duck pond in the village centre. A bigger pay and display car park is just on the edge of the village on the Warslow to Hulme End road.

Description

Hartington is a very popular Derbyshire village. It has everything a hotel with accommodation and cosy bar, a public house, pleasant tea rooms and shops to tempt the visitor. You will have plenty of time to sample these delights as this walk is short and relatively easy, starting with a climb up a minor road passing the youth hostel (with a tea room). The route then follows tracks to the top end of Biggin Dale. The grassy dale track and path take you to your next very short but steep path to a track that you follow back to the village.

Route Instructions

1. From the centre of the village walk back along the B5054 to pass the Beresford Tea Rooms and the Post Office. {A} Just before the telephone kiosk and by the brown YHA sign on the left, turn right up Hall Bank.

2. In about ½ mile and having passed the youth hostel, turn right signed "Biggin" onto cycle route 54. {B}

3. Follow this shale walled track for a mile. At the junction with the minor road (Dale End), keep straight on for another 100 metres then turn right.

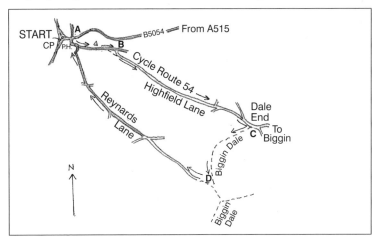

61

4. {C} Enter the top end of Biggin Dale. Follow the track then a path down the shallow wide dale for about ½ mile.

5. Just after going through a small gate in the wall ahead and at the footpath post, turn right to follow the Hartington route. {D}

6. Climb the short steep path to cross a stile by a gate.

7. Follow the gated track for about ½ mile to join a minor road (Reynards Lane) follow this lane back to Hartington, about ¾ mile.

WALK 22

Lud's Church (to the North West of The Roaches)

Bearstone Rock, Lud's Church, Forest Wood, Back Forest, Bearstone Rock

Map: Explorer OL24 White Peak
Start of the walk: SJ 978654
Distance: 3 miles
Approx. Time: 1 ½ hours
Grade: 1★
Paths: Woodland and moorland paths
Stiles: S
Refreshments: The Roaches Tea Rooms near Upper Hulme
Picnic: Near Lud's Church and SJ978654 area

Directions

From Leek take the A53 to Buxton. In 3 ½ miles turn left to Upper Hulme. Follow the narrow winding road, taking a left fork, down into and through Upper Hulme. Continue along the minor road passing the Roaches Tea Rooms and parking areas below The Roaches. In about 1 ½ miles and having gone through a gate you will reach another gate. Park where safe before or after the right hand bend round Bearstone Rock near Roach End.

Description

A short walk beyond the rocky edge of The Roaches with the magnificent awe inspiring Lud's Church reached by a flight of stone steps. The deep rocky cleft is about 100 metres long and only 2 metres wide. Over the years this cleft has offered shelter to many renegades. Robin Hood is thought to have used it. Followers of John Wycliff (a church reformer) used this remote cleft for worship in the 15th century, hence its current name. Soon after leaving Lud's Church a tall mound of rocks offer a suitable picnic area. The return route follows the gradually climbing moorland paths back to the start.

Route Instructions

1. The walk starts where the minor road bends round Bearstone Rock. Walk up the steps with your back to Bearstone Rock and The Roaches and track on the right. Go through a stile and immediately cross a stile on the right. {A}

2. Follow a wall on the right as you walk down the old stone and rocky path soon entering a wood. At the bottom of the path, cross a stream to walk up to a footpath post.

3. Turn left signed "Lud's Church & Swythamley". Follow the woodland path for about ¾ mile as it contours the hillside. At the next footpath post turn left to Lud's Church. At a fork of paths take the right hand path.

4. {B} When you reach the deep rock cleft of Lud's Church follow the left hand path which soon takes you down steps into the deep cleft. Follow the route through this awe inspiring natural rock cleft. This feature has been formed by a landslide, where a large section of rock has become detached from the hillside. As you walk through the 100 metres long narrow winding passage the moss and fern covered rock sides tower over 15 metres (50ft) above you.

5. Leave the cleft by a short flight of steps and turn left. At the next signpost keep straight on {C} following the clear moorland path, first in a westerly direction then turning south.

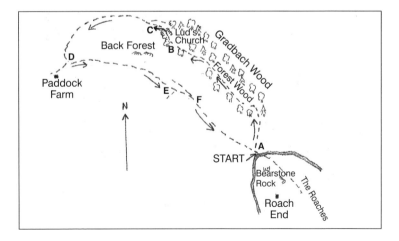

6. At a junction of paths {D} turn left signed Roach End. This a good picnic spot.

7. Follow the path below the Back Forest ridge keeping a wall on the right. In just over ¾ mile at a junction of paths continue ahead still following the Roach End route. {E} Go through a small gate. {F} At the next junction of paths, bear round to the right to continue in the same direction. After ½ mile go through a gate and back to the start of the walk.

WALK 23
The Roaches

The Roaches bus stop, Rockhall, The Roaches Edge, Bearstone Rock, Minor road

Map: Explorer OL24 White Peak
Parking: Grid Ref SK004622 (Week days only)
Distance: 4 miles
Approx. Time: 2 hours
Grade: 2*
Paths: Rocky edge paths and a minor road
Stiles: S
Refreshments: The Roaches Tea Rooms near Upper Hulme
Picnic: The Roaches

Directions

From Ashbourne take the Leek road. In the outskirts of Leek turn right then right again to follow the A53 Buxton road. In 3 ½ miles turn left to Upper Hulme. Follow the minor road through the village passing the tea rooms, aiming for the parking area along the road below the The Roaches. One of the earlier parking areas is reserved for disabled and this is where the walk starts.

Description

This is a stimulating walk which starts with an invigorating climb up onto the gritstone edge of The Roaches. The views from this rocky undulating path are magnificent. After a gradual descent from the edge you have a pleasant walk back along the quiet minor road again with far reaching views across to Tittesworth Reservoir.

Route Instructions

1. From where you park return to the disabled area and a farm gate and small gate. Go through the small gate and turn right up a gravel path for about 200 metres then turn left. {A}

2. Follow the path up to a wall which you follow for a few metres before going through a wall gap.

3. Keep straight on uphill with the wall of Rockhall on the right. At the old gate (Don Whillans), turn left continuing uphill and up the steep rock steps.

4. At the top turn left. Walk below the high rock outcrops then through open woodland for about 300 metres.

5. Turn right up the next steep rocky partly stepped path. At the top turn left.

6. {B} Follow the undulating rocky path across The Roaches.

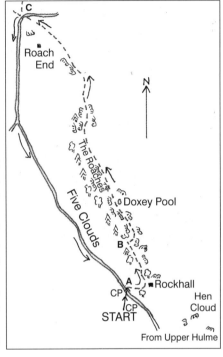

In about 400 metres you will pass Doxy Pool. From the pool to the minor road at the end of The Roaches, near Bearstone Rock, will take about 40 to 50 minutes continuous walking.

7. {C} Turn left to follow the quiet pleasant and gated minor road for nearly 1 ½ miles back to the parking area. The views from this road make it an enjoyable easy route at the end of the walk.

As you can see walks 22 and 23 could be combined to give a 7 mile walk.

WALK 24
Black Rocks and Wirksworth

Black Rocks Car Park, Bolehill, Wirksworth, High Peak Trail

Map: Explorer OL24 White Peak
Parking: Grid Ref SK 291557
Distance: 4 ½ miles
Approx. Time: 3 hours
Grade: 3*
Paths: Field paths and tracks and minor roads
Stiles: SS
Refreshments: Wirksworth, Middleton Top and Cromford

Directions

From Matlock take the A6 to Cromford. At the lights turn right onto the A5012 Newhaven road and in a few metres where it turns right keep straight on up the B5036. In ¾ mile turn left at the brown sign for Black Rocks. Follow the minor road, ignoring the first turn off left by the High Peak Trail notice, then just before the bridge and the 30mph sign turn left at the second HPT notice. Pass a small car parking area on the left and toilet block on the right to enter the larger car park.

Description

Although this is not in the Peak District it is a walk full of interest, variety and history with wonderful far reaching views, rewards for some of the steep ascents and descents. The walk through Wirksworth takes you through the little known areas of the town very rarely seen when driving through to reach other places. In September it is particularly interesting when the annual craft/ heritage celebrations are held (starting on the second weekend of the month). Also of interest are the Well Dressings starting on May Bank Holiday. If you wish you could start the walk at Middleton Top car park.

Route Instructions

1. From the top car park walk to the far end by the DCC Countryside notice board. Go through the gateway and across the trail.

2. Climb the wide stony track. Follow a wall on the right passing a small fenced enclosure on the left. Notice the towering massive rocks over to the left. The track soon bears round to the left where you continue on up through the trees ignoring all side

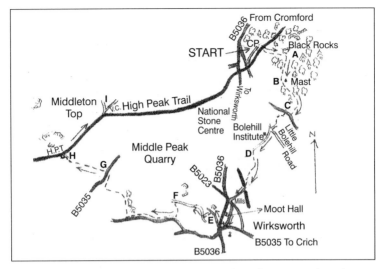

paths. Eventually you reach steps on the right. Climb up these passing through a gate partway up and then turn right to follow a fence on the right. {A} Continue on up a rocky path, ignoring a gate on the right, and still following the fence on the right. As you walk through the bracken and heather you will see the mast over to the left.

3. At the top, by the trig point {B} follow the fence on the right. Go through a gate and continue ahead through the scrub, bracken and pine trees. The path soon starts to descend through the wood.

4. At the "No Bicycles" sign cross the stile to leave the wood. Bear left down the field to cross a stile by two farm gates. Walk to and past the waymarked post then on down very steeply to the next waymarked post in the gorse bushes.

5. Follow the steep walled and fenced path downhill to go through a gated stile then a squeeze stile onto the road.

6. Turn right down the road for about 100 metres then turn left through a narrow wall gap. {C} Follow the narrow path passing through a stile then on down steps on a surfaced path passing Hillside Cottage. At the end of the path continue on downhill on a surfaced drive.

7. Pass the Methodist Church to cross Little Bolehill road. Continue on down a rough road in the same direction (no through road). Pass Bolehill Institute 1889.

8. At the end of the road keep straight on down a fenced track. {D} After passing an old barn you will be on a narrow path with old fencing. At the end of this path, go

through a gate.

9. Turn right to follow a clear path across two fields. Go through a gate and across a bridge to walk up a road passing North End Mills.

10. At the road junction just before the main road turn left signed "Whatstandwell and Crich". In a few metres and opposite "The Old Lock Up" turn right up Chapel Lane. Pass the Charles Bathurst building which is a Moot Hall built in 1814 where the Barmote Court met to deal with lead mining matters.

11. When you reach the chapel you can turn right for the toilets then a few metres further on you can turn left for a coffee shop and right to continue the walk.

12. At the junction with the main B5036 road through Wirksworth by the market place keep straight on across the road. Walk up the narrow steep Dale End hill for a few metres. Ignore the hill off left to walk up the very steep Greenhill. Just passed Babbington House on the left turn left before the top of the hill.{E}

13. Walk up the narrow surfaced path with a hand rail on the left. From the top of this jitty you have wonderful views over Wirksworth. This path brings you down to a minor road where you turn right.

14. Follow this fascinating road with its sides guarded by rampart like walls. After the last house continue on up the minor road. Just before a small parking area and pole steps turn left up a fenced path.{F}

15. The path takes you through scrubland, past old quarry workings and through an old tunnel.

16. After climbing a short hill, walk parallel to the road for nearly ½ mile going through four gates, passing a small stone barn, then through a low squeeze stile and the fifth gate. At the end of this section walk up a wide grass track (narrow field) immediately after a right-hand bend go through a wide wall gap on the left. Keep straight on across three fields and two more gaps.

17. In the third field turn right by the waymarked post. You now have a wood on the right as you walk down the field going through another gap. At the bottom of the field, turn left by the waymarked post.

18. Walk to and through the stile ahead. Turn right to follow the old wall on the right. Go through a squeeze stile in the field corner. Keep straight on passing an old farm gate to go through another squeeze stile. Keep the field boundary close on the left in the next field. Turn left in the field corner to cross a stile then the road and another stile. {G}

19. Keep straight on across the middle of the next three fields crossing a stile and a small gate. In the third field you will have a broken wall on the right. At a wall-corner head for the stile and steps ahead. Cross the stile then up the steps and path ahead to

join a wide track. {H}

20. Turn left then in a few metres turn right back on yourself to go through a small gate by a farm gate onto The High Peak Trail. Follow the trail for about 1 ½ miles, passing the Visitor Centre at Middleton Top, back to Black Rocks Car Park.

WALK 25
Cromford and High Peak Trail

Arkwright Mill Car Park, Cromford Wharf and Canal, High Peak Junction, High Peak Trail, Dene Quarry, Cromford

Map: Explorer OL24 White Peak
Parking: Grid Ref SK299570
Distance: 5 ½ miles
Approx. Time: 3 hours
Grade: 2
Paths: Surfaced and shady canal paths, trails and narrow woodland paths
Stiles: S
Refreshments: Café at Arkwright Mill, Inns in Cromford
Picnic: Cromford Wharf, High Peak Junction, Instruction 4
Toilets: Arkwright Mill

Directions

From Matlock take the A6 south to Cromford and Derby. After 2 ½ miles, at the cross roads and lights in Cromford, turn left down Mill Road signed Lea, Holloway, Crich and Arkwright's Mill. In 300 metres turn left into the Mill Car Park.

Description

This is a walk for a warm summer afternoon. The pretty flat canal path, then the steady climb up the dramatic rock bordered High Peak Trail provide shade for the start of the walk. The return route to Cromford follows woodland scrub and quarry edge paths. There are a number of inns in Cromford if you want an evening meal.

Route Instructions

1. Leave the car park via the main entrance and turn left. After about 100 metres turn

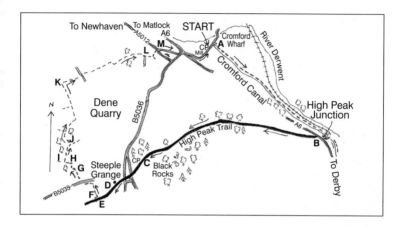

right to enter the Cromford Wharf car park {A} where you join the canal path on your right.

2. With the canal on the right walk along the path for just over 1 mile.

3. Turn right over the canal at the High Peak Junction. Pass the picnic tables and turn right to walk behind the visitor centre passing the old railway rolling stock. {B} Walk up the trail passing under the A6.

4. Follow the High Peak Trail for nearly a mile to go through a gate and pass the Sheep Pasture Engine House. From here the trail flattens out. Pass Black Rock car park, {C} Steeple Grange Lt. Railway {D} and the first sign to The National Stone Centre.

5. At the second sign to the stone centre (which is on the right), turn right {E} to leave the trail having followed it for 2 miles.

6. Turn right to walk through a car park and at the road turn left. {F} If you wish to visit the stone centre follow the blue signs.

7. At the junction with the B5035 turn left to follow a short path parallel to the road then cross the road at the footpath sign. Cross a cattle grid to follow a track for a few metres and immediately after crossing a small bridge turn left to leave the track. {G}

8. Walk down a bank to follow an undulating winding path through the hummocky area of old mine workings. There are a number of paths on this small area so keep to the main path with a wall on left. **Do not go to the end of the wall where there is an old gateway** but bear off right where the broken wall bends left by an old single hawthorn tree. Almost immediately turn left to walk to and through the bushes to cross a squeeze stile. {H}

9. Follow the fence on the right for a few metres then turn right to cross through the post stile on the right {I} following the field boundary on the left. In the field corner turn left to enter a wood.

10. Crossing a wooden squeeze stile to continue along the woodland path. Next you will walk through a scrub area and across an open area with an old stone barn up on the right.

11. {J} At a wooden stile ahead (**do not cross it**) turn left down a wooded path with the quarry on the right. At the top of a short climb you come to a T-junction of paths, turn right to follow a path above the quarry, parts of which have been reinforced with chippings.

12. Enter an undulating woodland route which you leave via a flight of steps. Stay on the fenced path following the quarry on the right and ignoring a path on the left. Eventually the path goes round a right-hand corner with a wall on the left. {K}

13. At the end of this path turn left through a squeeze stile then through a small gate. In a few metres turn right through a wall gap and walk across a quarry track to go over a stile.

14. Keep straight on with the field boundary on the right. Near the field corner bear off left by a stone gatepost to cross a low wall gap. Continue in the same direction, with old mining walls on the right.

15. Enter a tree-lined old walled track. At the bottom of the first section of this track go through a small metal gate to continue down the track.

16. Eventually you will reach the first houses in Cromford. Cross the end of a metalled road {L} to keep straight on down the track. When you reach a surfaced footpath ahead turn left through a low stile.

17. With a fence on the right walk steeply down to the road.

18. Cross the road to {M} Scarthin and turn right to walk up this narrow one-way road. Pass the well known Scarthin Book Shop on the left and a lake and The Boat Inn on the right.

19. Join the B5012 and turn left. Cross the B5012 and the A6 via the pedestrian crossings. Walk down Mill Road back to Arkwright Mill Car Park.

WALK 26

Darley Bridge and Wensley Dale

Darley Bridge, Derwent Heritage Way, Wensley Dale, Wensley, Clough Wood, Oldfield Lane, Darley Bridge

Map: Explorer OL 24 White Peak
Parking: Grid Ref SK 271620
Distance: 4 miles
Approx. Time: 2 hours
Grade: 1
Paths: Field and woodland paths and tracks
Stiles: SS
Refreshments: Darley Bridge

Directions

From Matlock travel northwards along the A6 for about 2 ½ miles and after passing DFS turn left along the B5057 Winster road. In just over ½ mile cross the Derwent River into Darley Bridge and immediately turn left to a small parking area on the left-hand side of the road.

Description

A varied walk best followed after a period of dry weather. The Derwent Valley Heritage Way provides you with an easy flat start before you walk up the gentle slope of the wide grassy Wensley Dale. There are a few picnic spots towards the end of the dale. From Wensley you descend quite steeply through Clough Wood where it can be quite wet. The return route down Oldfield Lane takes you back to Darley Bridge where the "Three Stags Head" is a welcome refreshment stop.

Route Instructions

1. From the parking area turn left to follow the Derwent Valley Heritage Way. You will pass through 2 stiles (or gates) staying on the main surfaced track across the meadows. After the second stile bear up right to pass a barn on the right. Soon the track becomes a minor road with property on the right. {A} Opposite "The Firs" bungalow and nearly a mile from the start turn left off the minor road.

2. Walk down the hedged path to the river. Cross a small stone footbridge and continue along the riverside path going through two small gates and a stile. {B} Just before a wooden step stile turn right back on yourself.

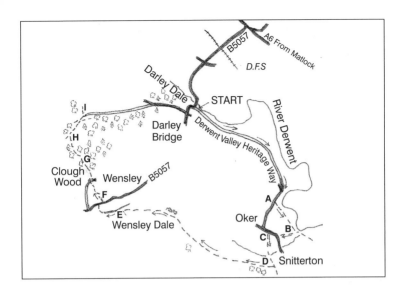

3. Cross the field to the opposite hedge and cross the stile. Turn right along the road and just before the "Oker" sign turn left over the stile. {C}

4. Keep straight on with the hedge close on the left. Cross a stile in the field corner then go through a gateway crossing a stone slab. Walk towards the village and at the footpath sign turn right to follow the Wensley route. {D}

5. Keep a wall close on the left and where it bends left continue ahead aiming for a gate and waymarked stile in the fence ahead. Cross the stile and keep straight on to cross another stile where the old wall meets a fence.

6. Bear left up the next field aiming for a single hawthorn tree. Cross the stile by this tree. Continue ahead first with a wall on the left then on the right after crossing another stile.

7. Continue up the dale keeping the old wall on the right. Pass through a farm gate/gateway, the wall is now on the left for a few metres and where it turns left keep straight on aiming for a small gate to the left of the rock outcrops (this may be slightly hidden in the summer).

8. Go through the gate to continue up the wide dale. Here there are possible picnic spots if the ground has dried out! Cross a gated stile by a farm gate.

9. After about a mile from the Wensley footpath sign you will join a shale track where you turn left. {E} Walk towards and past the cottages. Just after the cottages go through

a small gate on the right.

10. Walk up the winding stepped path to the road in Wensley. Turn right for a few metres then turn left at the footpath sign to Clough Wood. {F}

11. Follow the field boundary close on the right which soon turns round to the left to have a fence on the right. Pass a pond on the left and aim for a small gate. Go through the gate, across the drive and through another small gate.

12. Turn right to follow the fence then the wood close on the right. Cross the stile in the field corner. {G}

13. Follow the woodland path, at first down steps, which winds downhill through woodland then across a more open area where you pass a waymarked sign on the left and a pond on the right. As you enter a more wooded area the path becomes quite steep and would be muddy and very wet after heavy rain.

14. Eventually the path flattens out and you pass under power line supports before crossing a footbridge. {H} At a T-junction of tracks turn right uphill, continuing following the power lines.

15. After passing the boom turn right down a track {I} turning right again at the T-junction.

16. Continue down the surfaced track to join a minor road where you turn right to walk down into Darley Bridge.

17. At the road junction in the village you will see the inn. To return to the parking area turn left.

WALK 27
High Peak Junction and Cromford Canal

High Peak Junction Car Park, Cromford Canal, Whatstandwell, Midshires Way, Watergate Farm, Intake Lane

Map: Explorer OL24 White Peak
Parking: Grid Ref SK 315561
Distance: 5 miles
Approx. Time: 2 ½ to 3 hours
Grade: 2
Paths: Tow path, field paths and tracks
Stiles: SS

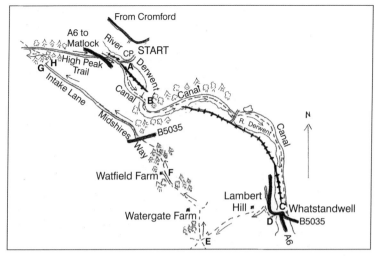

Refreshments: Snacks High Peak Junction (not always open) Cromford Mill and Whatstandwell

Picnic: High Peak Junction and Instruction 18

Directions

From Matlock take the A6 south to Cromford. At the traffic lights in Cromford turn left to Arkwright Mill. Drive past the mills and the church to cross the River Derwent. Ignore a road off left to follow the river on your right for about 1 ½ miles. Turn right into High Peak Junction Car Park.

Description

This is a pleasant and stimulating walk. It is in both a beautiful river valley and a treasure house of early Industrial Revolution which was a time of much activity and energy. As well as walking by the canal and river you have a taste of the undulating Midshires Way.

Route Instructions

1. From the car park walk to the southern end to cross the bridge over the River Derwent then on up to cross the railway. {A} At the canal (not across the bridge) turn left, signed Leewood Pump and Ambergate, to walk along the towpath with the canal on your right.

2. In about ¼ mile the canal crosses the river then a little further on you cross the canal {B} to continue along the path with the canal now on your left. After 2 miles from

High Peak Junction and having gone through 3 tunnels you will leave the towpath to walk up to the B5035 in Whatstandwell. {C}

3. Turn right to walk down to the A6 and across the bridge. At the end of the bridge cross and leave the A6 to keep straight on towards and over a stile. {D}

4. Walk up the field to cross a road via two stiles.

5. Follow a path at the edge of a wood with a wall on the right. In about 100 metres turn left to follow The Derwent Valley Walk. Walk up the hill with your back to the A6.

6. Join a surfaced track for a few metres before turning left to follow a fence close on the right. Cross two stiles passing "Lambert Hill".

7. Keep straight on up the next four fields following the field boundaries on the left and crossing a stile, a gate and a wide hedge gap.

8. {E} At a crossing of paths do NOT go through the stile but turn right downhill keeping the wood on your left and aiming for a house on the hillside ahead. You are now on the Midshires Way.

9. Cross a stile in the field corner to continue downhill to Watergate Farm. Go through a small gate to cross a paddock diagonally then over a stile. Cross the farm drive to walk along a walled path then follow a stream on the left before climbing up through a wood.

10. Cross a stile and bear slightly right up the field to cross another stile hidden behind a hawthorn and elder tree. Continue uphill to the wall to cross a stile in the field corner by a farm gate. (Not the stile on the left)

11. Walk uphill to join a track and turn left to walk to and past the houses. {F} At Watfield Farm, go through a stile by a farm gate then leave the track to follow a path on the right.

12. Walk uphill to cross two stiles and a gate passing the farm buildings on your left.

13. Cross a waymarked stile to walk along the edge of a wood. Soon you will walk through and down the conifer wood, ignore a permissive path on the right. At the end of the wood, cross two stiles to walk diagonally down the field and across a stile in the field corner.

14. Cross the road to follow the Public Bridleway sign.

15. You will now follow a partly surfaced track (Intake Lane) for about ¾ mile passing a caravan site.

16. {G} At a conifer wood and a wall ahead turn right to pass by a metal gate. Follow a wooded walled track which shortly goes round a left bend. {H} (Picnic area) Continue on downhill through the woods.

17. At a waymarked post take the left fork uphill signed "High Peak Trail". At the junction with the High Peak Trail turn right.

18. Walk down the trail for about ¾ mile back to High Peak Junction where you cross the canal to retrace your outward route back to the car park.

WALK 28
Matlock and Bonsall

Matlock Car Park, Snitterton Road, Upperwood, Bonsall, Ember Lane, Heights of Abraham, Masson Lees Farm, Matlock

Map: Explorer OL 24 White Peak
Parking: SK297602
Distance: 5 miles
Approx. Time: 2 ½ to 3 hours
Grade: 3★
Stiles: SS
Refreshments: Matlock and Bonsal
Picnic: Instruction 15

Directions

Matlock is on the A6 north of Derby. Park in the main town car park in Matlock, off the A6 and between the station and Sainsburys.

Description

This is the most stimulating walk in the book. The field and woodland paths and tracks and minor roads across the hillsides above Matlock and Matlock Bath give wonderful views and are a reward for the climbs. Camera and binoculars are recommended equipment.

Route Instructions

1. From the car park return to the A6 and immediately turn right up Snitterton Road for a few metres then bear off left at the footpath sign. {A}
2. Walk up the steep narrow road passing Bridge Farm. Climb the steps to go through the squeeze stile. Walk up the field ahead to a waymarked post.
3. At the post, bear off left to cross the stile in the wall ahead. Continue in the same direction across two fields, two stiles and a gate, then turn left.
4. Follow a wall on the left downhill. Shortly you bear away from the wall to walk on

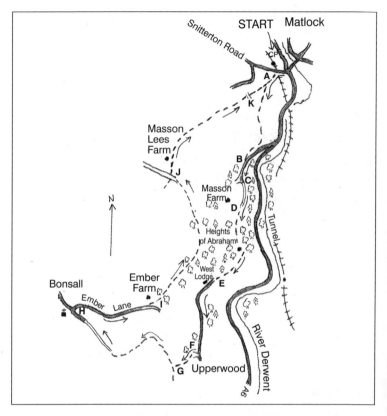

an unfenced winding grass track contouring the open wooded hillside before reaching the wall again on the left.

5. Keep the wall on your left and a high wooded bank on the right. Join a lane and turn right. {B}

6. Walk up the rather steep lane passing the chapel up on the right. In about 200 metres at a fork of lanes bear left signed "Public footpath No 69 to Matlock Bath". Go through the gate/gateway. {C}

7. Continue along the wide track with a high wall on the right. At the private road sign on a farm gate to Masson Farm {D} bear off down left still on the Matlock Bath route. The woodland path soon starts to climb via a series of steps. Eventually you will pass under the cable car lines, after which the path gradually descends via one bridge

and a flight of steps to the minor road. {E}

8. Turn right up the steep road passing West Lodge and the ticket office for The Heights of Abraham. As you climb the road enjoy the wide reaching views.

9. At a fork in the road, {F} turn right uphill to a turning circle. Go through a stile on the left of a metal gate on the left. Follow the wide woodland path. Cross a concrete track to continue uphill on a wooded path. Go through a squeeze stile.

10. Keep straight on across the field to cross another squeeze stile. {G} Turn right up a track, which soon becomes a path.

11. Walk between the hawthorn bushes and on up the field with the quarry boundary on the left. Pass through a gateway and continue down the track and round a left-hand bend then on down the track, going through gates/ gateways to join the surfaced road into Bonsall.

12. {H} In about ¼ mile opposite the church turn right.

13. Walk up Ember Lane going through a farm gate. Just after passing Ember Farm on the left leave the lane to go through a stile on the left signed "Public footpath to Matlock". {I} Ignore a path off right to keep to the higher woodland path.

14. Eventually you cross a track which leads down into The Heights of Abraham where there are facilities. (Open weekends only in the winter, late autumn and early spring. Rest of the year open daily)

15. Follow the fence on the right round the site. Turn right through a rocky area to a surfaced path where you turn left uphill. (This is a good picnic area) Follow the winding path up through the rocky then woodland areas. Pass a telescope to follow the green arrow sign up on the left. The path winds uphill to join a track behind the viewing platform.

16. Continue along the stony track for about ¼ mile and just before another uphill section turn right opposite a stile on the left to go through a stile by a farm gate. {J}

17. Walk down the field to follow the hawthorn trees on the right. Go through a small gate by a farm gate. Walk diagonally down the next field to cross a stile in the field corner.

18. Follow the field boundary on the right and keep straight on until you see a broken wall, a hidden low stile and a gateway across a farm track on the left. Go through this gateway. Keeping the field boundary on the right, continue in the same direction crossing 3 fields and 3 stiles.

19. Walk through a small copse to cross a stile then on down the field, through an old gateway and over a stile. Turn right following a short wooded path to cross a track and through another stile. {K}

20. Walk down the steep field passing the waymarked post of your outward route. Retrace your outward route back to the car park.

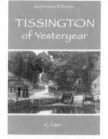
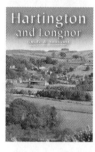

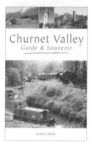